Women & Thru-Hiking on the Appalachian Trail

practical advice from hundreds of women long distance hikers

BY

Beverly "Maine Rose" Hugo

DISCARD

ISBN 1-889386-31-6

Women & Thru-Hiking on the Appalachian Trail
practical advice from hundreds of women long distance hikers

Library of Congress Cataloging in Publication Data

Published by:

Appalachian Trail Conference
799 Washington Street
P.O. Box 807
Harpers Ferry, WV 25425
<www.appalachiantrail.com>

Cover Design By: Douglas Graphics

ISBN 1-889386-31-6

Dedication

To my son, Raviv Ramdial, for his mellow temperament and adaptable nature. To my adventurous daughter, Saretta Ramdial, for her bravery, courage, and determined spirit. To my sisters, Candace Alper, Ruth-Anne Hugo, and Janice Hugo Martino for their love, support, and encouragement before, during, and after the hike.

Rosie Comments

Researching this book has involved a process of individual and group personal growth and exploration. In thru-hiking the Appalachian Trail, we deal in quantifiable variables: daily mileage, months on the Trail, calories consumed, pounds and ounces of packweight, number of blisters, letters received, and pounds lost...and alas, gained back. However, this is not a controlled quantitative study despite conclusions we drew from the survey and questionnaire sent to hundreds of women 2000 milers, thru-hikers, and long distance section hikers.

The hallmark of this project is the use of multiple qualitative research methods. We wanted to tap the expertise of women of varying ages, backgrounds, and hiking experience. Yet, we also wanted to write a book that speaks to the novice woman hiker contemplating a traditional thru-hike of the Appalachian Trail from terminus to terminus, end-to-end.

Our sample represents the traditional thru-hiking community: American, white, middle-class, college educated. The voices of African-American women and other minorities are present but infrequent. We are eager to include the personal responses of all women who have long distance backpacking experience on the AT and welcome their participation in future editions of this book.

Many women, especially women over 40, have not had the exposure, been allowed to participate, or had the opportunity to be involved in competitive sports or other physically demanding activities. Many now are making up for lost time. Women reading this book may even remember when girls were not allowed to play baseball in Little League or run in the Boston Marathon or when they were not considered physically capable of playing full court basketball. Thanks to Title 9 and the feminist movement, there have been great inroads in expanding athletic choices for girls and women. Young women may not even realize that the many opportunities now available for them are the result of long fought battles on and off the playing field and should not take their present good fortune for granted.

Most women have not gone to war or spent years in competitive situations demanding the resourcefulness thought necessary for a successful thru-hike. However, women are excellent planners. Women with families are experts at organizing and juggling dozens of responsibilities. When things get difficult in a family, they still do the chores, get up with sick kids, and hold down the fort at home and at work. They also like to walk and a thru-hike is a lot of walking albeit over lots of difficult terrain. If women can understand the similarities drawn from home and career challenges, they can successfully "transition" the skills and talents from their regular lives to the tasks necessary to thru-hike the Appalachian Trail.

Many women have never consciously chosen an "elective" challenge of a physical nature. An elective challenge can be physical, emotional, spiritual, or intellectual. A thru-hike, although seemingly physical in nature, can be a total benefit for the individual's mind, body, and spirit. It is a non-competitive endeavor that can stretch a woman in directions she never thought possible. This is the gift a thru-hike can give if a woman is willing to accept it.

In the spring of '97 Dan Wingfoot Bruce, www.trailplace.com website founder and administrator, asked the WATL (Women's Appalachian Trail List-a women only listserve) if someone would like to undertake coordinating a women's book project. Although WATL is no longer on Trailplace, list members have regrouped as WomenHikers on www.onelist.com.

My immediate decision to volunteer was as determined as the decision to thru-hike. This would be a unique undertaking, a project conceived and developed on-line with no real precedent. It would demand the cooperation of women who had never met and the result would be a collaborative effort by women long distance AT hikers throughout the country.

I also didn't have a clue where to begin. After thru-hiking the AT with practically no previous experience, I certainly wasn't going to let a lack of knowledge about book editing get in my way. I needed to make the contacts with other women AT hikers on-line, at hiking conferences and get togethers, through gathering names and addresses from several directories, and from women participants in my AT programs throughout the country.

I spoke with Wingfoot for a brief few minutes outside Ramsey's Deli in Hot Springs, North Carolina during my '95 thru-hike. Little did I know that a few years later we would be working together on an AT women's project. It soon became clear to me through weekly phone conversations and e-mails that Wingfoot had a vision of the needs of novice women hikers. He also had a compassion for women who have reservations about their ability to undertake a thru-hike. This thread of understanding was always at the forefront of his mind. That helped me realize that not every woman is going to approach a thru-hike with the same confidence and self-assuredness that I had. He helped me quickly understand what he had gleaned from many years of conversations with hundreds of women throughout the country. We never lost track of the importance of this project for thousands of potential AT long distance women hikers.

For a year and a half we compiled data through several channels including hundreds of e-mails, an on-line bulletin board, and subsequent 72-question database. In late April '98, I presented a slide show and talk at the Hot Springs Trailfest celebrating 50 years of thru-hiking. I spent two weeks in that North Carolina mountain town discussing the project with Wingfoot for countless hours at the Smoky Mountain Diner. I met and talked with women hikers as they passed through town. I collected their names and listened to their stories at the pancake breakfast, the campground, during the parade, at picnic tables, and of course, always back at the diner. Toward the end of the two weeks we were ready to send out the survey and lengthy questionnaire. We did not ask any questions about race, ethnic background, or religious affiliation. In the future, we hope to reach hundreds of other long distance women AT hikers through responses to the book that will add to our growing treasury of women's observations and contributions.

Returning to Maine, I eagerly called to Wingfoot to check on the survey and questionnaire responses. Who could have anticipated the response from women I had never even met? These are women who put themselves in physically and mentally demanding situations for months. They understood what we needed, reliving their own hikes in the process. I was overwhelmed with the honesty of their comments. Many searched deep within their hearts, minds, and souls in expressing what the Trail meant to them. We intentionally demanded a lot with our lengthy non-traditional research questionnaire. Women realized the importance of their individual contributions often writing pages of extensive remarks. Long distance women backpackers do not always fit the norm. A neat little questionnaire would not suit our needs nor express theirs. A commonality of response emerged in many areas as we had already expected. Both Wingfoot and I knew that neither of us, nor any other single individual, could speak to all the concerns of novice women hikers. Instead we would let the experience of many 2000 milers, thru-hikers, and section hikers speak for itself.

On returning to Hot Springs in July '98, I started compiling the data for its final form. Surveys and questionnaire responses were still arriving at the Hot Springs post office throughout late summer and into the fall and were added to the later stages of the book. After the introductory chapter, the main body of the book is divided into three sections representing time periods critical to a thorough understanding of the thru-hiking experience: before, during, and after. This is not a how-to manual. Please refer to the excellent bibliography developed by Linda Patton, Earthworm, reference librarian at Florida State University in Tallahassee. I thank the many women who have shared their AT hikes for being so supportive of this unique long-range project and special thanks to Wingfoot for his mentoring and sense of humor. A complete list of contributors and supportive individuals is listed at the back of the book.

Happy Trails,
  Rosie

Please send your comments, questions, and Trail stories for use in future editions to:

Beverly "Maine Rose" Hugo
HIT THE TRAIL!
P.O. Box 6676
Portland, ME 04101
E-mail- hittrail@aol.com

Table of Contents

Introduction

The women you will read about in the following pages have hiked well over a quarter of a million miles on the Appalachian Trail. Some thru-hiked the entire 2,160 miles in one continuous journey from Georgia to Maine or Maine to Georgia following every white blaze with a pack on their back. Others section-hiked taking from 2 to 22 years to become 2000 milers. Many covered the distance scheduling their hikes around other areas of their lives or around recovery from trail injuries. The injured often returned in resourceful triumph. A few were teenagers when they went end-to-end while others were over 60. Some had more than ten years experience; others had none. Several hiked the AT twice. Many went on to hike other trails or undertake other challenges. They hiked solo, with partners, and in small groups. Some hiked with husbands, some not. Still others met future life partners on the Trail.

Many experienced a flowering of personal growth often simplifying their off Trail lives. These women hiked for their love of nature, for the pleasure of walking in the woods and on the mountain ridges, and to be part of the mystique of the Appalachian Trail. Many were in transition seeking change. Some looked for a challenge that would enhance their self-esteem and stretch their mental and physical abilities to new limits. The Trail was a spiritual journey for many, a life enhancing experience for all providing a wealth of lifetime friendships. Their honest reflections are representative of many hundreds if not thousands of other women who have also been called to follow this footpath for "Those who seek fellowship with the wilderness."

Early Women Appalachian Trail Hikers
Role Models Past and Present

From its inception and before its official completion in 1937, women have hiked the Appalachian Trail. Dr. Mary Kilpatrick was the first woman 2000 miler finishing in 1939. Over an eight-year period in the 1930's, Mary, her husband, and their friend, George W. Outerbridge, hiked the Appalachian

Trail in sections. Outerbridge wrote in recounting their many hikes, "Both the Kilpatricks have really uncanny noses for a trail; if there is the vestige of a rusty, battered-up old Appalachian Trail marker, or an almost faded-out paint blaze, half hidden in foliage, within a half mile of the last one, they will surely find it (Hare, James R., ed. Hiking the Appalachian Trail, Rodale Press, 1975, pg. 31)!"

In 1952 Mildred Lamb was the second woman to complete the Trail accompanied by her husband Dick. They hiked from Mt. Ogelthorpe in Georgia to the Susquehanna River and then flip flopped hiking south from Katahdin back to the Susquehanna.

It is Grandma Gatewood, however, who captures most hikers' imaginations with her two traditional thru-hikes and one section hike. Emma Gatewood was a colorful character. A former farm wife, she was an unimposing 5'2", weighed 155 pounds, and had given birth to 11 children. Like many women thru-hikers, Grandma first heard of the Trail by reading a magazine article. Her first attempt in 1954 came to an end after 24 miles and losing herself in the Maine woods. Grandma was not daunted by this setback. She returned the following year as the first woman to thru-hike the entire Appalachian Trail in one continuous journey from terminus to terminus.

She was 67 years old and carried a denim bag with about 20 pounds of gear. She cooked over an open fire, lost 30 pounds, wore out five pairs of sneakers, and hiked alone. "Grandma always hiked by herself, rarely going with others for more than a mile or two. She was comfortable only at her own pace, which included frequent pauses for rest, but was steady and generally began at five-thirty or six in the morning and kept on till three or four in the afternoon (Hare, pg. 62)." Grandma didn't worry about keeping her family posted, used a guidebook on only one occasion, and was quite content with eating cold food if necessary. She knew how to take care of herself. On all three hikes she never carried a tent, sleeping bag, or regular frame backpack. She was also the first person, man or woman, to hike the entire Trail a second time.

Grandma Gatewood's section hike spanned a ten year period. At the age of 77 she completed that hike and topped it off with an added ascent of Katahdin and a walk across the challenging Knife's Edge. She hiked with a flourish and completed many other trails throughout the United States. According to her daughter, Lucy, in a conversation with Dan "Wingfoot" Bruce, she boarded a Greyhound Bus with an excursion pass shortly before her death at age 85 and visited all of the lower 48 states. She just wanted to see new places and visit friends along the way. Grandma was a determined independent woman ahead of her time.

Like Grandma Gatewood, Dorothy Laker first heard about the Trail by reading an account of a hike. Dorothy thru-hiked twice, in 1957 and 1964. She section hiked a third time over the ten-year period between 1962 and 1972. Dorothy ordered trail maps, guidebooks, and food, and found herself a hiking partner. Her partner for her first hike backed out at the last minute. A friend who was supposed to send her packages to post offices along the Trail also reneged on that responsibility. She solved the shipping problem and left alone for Mt. Ogelthorpe, the original southern terminus of the Appalachian Trail.

She writes, "Down an old dirt road I could make out the first white paint blazes of the Trail. Now I suddenly began to feel the excitement of getting under way. In my mind I could picture the unbroken chain of white blazes, linking me firmly to Mt. Katahdin in Maine. Any step I took from this point on would diminish by just that much the distance remaining. Already the 2,000 miles ahead seemed less formidable. I took official possession- this was my Trail and I was on my way (Hare, pg. 68)."

Women have always been active in the organization of the Trail and have played key roles in Trail Clubs performing thousands of hours of administration and trail maintenance. However, it was Jean Cashin, official Trail Mom, who encouraged so many thru-hikers both on the phone and as they stopped at the ATC Headquarters in Harper's Ferry, the psychological halfway point of the Appalachian Trail. She was always there with a kind word and a big hug. In fact, the author received 14 of these hugs during the 14 unused takes of a Trailside PBS entry that never made it to production!

Grandma Gatewood, Dorothy Laker, and a number of other women past and present have served as role models for the women involved in this collaborative book project. These women, in turn, also serve as examples of women's capabilities in the outdoors.

Martha Manzano, Gypsy, first heard about Grandma Gatewood in the 70's. "I decided someday I would follow in her footsteps. She has been my hero all these years, a woman with spunk enough to do what she wanted to do. You can imagine how her family must have tried to talk her out of it, but she just set out with the bare necessities and none of the hi-tech stuff we have today."

Verna Soule, Gran'ma Soule, expresses a great admiration for Dorothy Laker. She read her Trail account over and over again and felt that Dorothy had a love for hiking and could handle anything that came up. Gran'ma Soule began hiking at the age of 50, has two thru-hikes to her credit, and was one of the featured hikers in a video about senior citizens thru-hiking the Long Trail in Vermont. She is now 73 and has hiked all over the United States with over 11,000 miles of trail under her feet.

Deb Blick, Cricket, on the Trail in '98, felt that Dorothy Laker's story spoke to her in a very personal way. Deb's mother, however, was her main role model. "When I wanted to be a Girl Scout and no one else's mom would volunteer to be our leader, my mom did. We had some great times together as I was growing up and many of them were spent in the woods on camping trips."

"I didn't have any female role models," writes Dania Egedi, Lightweight. "My father started me backpacking when I was nine. In fact, my first hike was up Blood Mountain in Georgia in December. The trip was completely miserable, but I loved it, and figured it couldn't get much worse than that. And, for the most part, I was right. Most everything that I learned about hiking and living outdoors came from my father."

Connie Salzarulo, Gladrags, is a future thru-hiker and has had the opportunity to actually hike with her role model and benefit from her knowledge. "Mary Sands, Mama Boots, has the wonderful ability to make people feel comfortable and to instill the confidence needed for hiking over mountains." Mama Boots is the author of the Appalachian Trail in Bits and Pieces describing her 20-year hiking history with the Girl Scouts.

Linda Ivey, Mountain Mama, began section hiking the Trail in 1994 after calling Mama Boots for encouragement and receiving an invitation to hike on the next group venture. "We only hiked 20 miles in 2 1/2 days but it was the most painful struggle imaginable. On the third day she literally had to walk behind me and encourage me each step. If I had had a gun, I would have shot her! Thank goodness I didn't, because several days later I was able to appreciate what she had done for me. She never once raised her voice or seemed to give up." Linda has now hiked over 1000 miles of the AT. She works with Girl Scouts, and encourages beginners on their initial forays on the Trail.

Prolific writer, Cindy Ross, is a role model for many women hikers who have read accounts of her trials and tribulations on a number of trails all over the United States. Christine Shaw, Firefly, writes that Cindy's stories gave her courage and made her believe she could do it. Ginny Owen, Spirit Walker, admires Cindy for her openness about her emotions in her books. "She made me feel that it was okay to be emotional while hiking. Fear and loneliness may be part of the experience, but so is joy and happiness, and none of them will keep me from doing what I want and need to do."

Susanne Wright Ashland has met several older women who have influenced her. "Since I started hiking I have met a couple of women who have served as inspiration to me. I have each of their pictures on my fridge. The first I met on the top of Double Top in Baxter State Park. She celebrated her 70th birthday that day and had been backpacking the hundred-mile wilderness with her grandson and now was doing this mountain. The second was at Chimney Pond; she was 73. That is part of what I want in my life. To stay active and healthy and hike mountains when I am in my 70's and 80's. I would like to be that kind of inspiration to other women."

During the '98 Trailfest celebration, the author had the opportunity to eat at Elmer's Inn in Hot Springs. Hikers and other guests took every seat at the two large dining room tables as each answered the traditional question of the evening and dined on superb vegetarian fare. After dinner several women hikers looked over the survey and questionnaire and one young woman, Amity Clifford, Dutchboy, dashed from the room to go upstairs. She quickly returned with an old black and white photo portraying three women dressed for the outdoors in quite another era. Amity carries this photo with her at all times and it is especially meaningful for her on her thru-hike. One of the women in the picture is Amity's grandmother in her younger years. She was among the first women to thru-hike the Long Trail in Vermont. This photo serves as an inspiration and her grandmother's spirit is with her at all times.

Other hikers mention chance encounters with women on the Trail whose presence and determination they admire and emulate. But Nancy Marth, Geo, states a fact true for many women involved in this project. "I did not have any hiking role models and it didn't occur to me to wish I had. I knew that gender was no basis for a successful thru-hike and I felt that the information already out there was sufficient."

Many women have discovered a new, more vibrant voice since successfully completing their thru-hikes or venturing onto the Trail for long distances. They have continued living their Trail experience by creatively sharing it with others in public or in private and thus, in their own turn, becoming role models for others. The Trail has produced or enhanced the contributions of authors, free lance writers, motivational speakers, school curriculum innovators, trip organizers, Girl Scout leaders, and more environmentally responsible individuals.

Women bring their strengths, insights, and resourcefulness to their friends, families, communities and to whatever endeavor and new challenge they decide to undertake. They have remained in contact with the Trail by becoming active in the ATC-Appalachian Trail Conference, local hiking clubs, and other Trail organizations. They are involved in trail maintenance, ridge running, shelter or hostel caretaking, conference planning, and hiking seminars. They serve by example. You can, too. Start now.

Chapter one

BEFORE

What age and experience qualifications do women need to thru-hike?

Many women rose to the occasion, as was entirely predicted, expressing strong feelings that one need not be a certain age or have any special experience to thru-hike. Many had recommendations that would ease the process. Some expressed the opinion that having camping and backpacking experience is essential. Our survey results show that many successful women thru-hikers have completed the Trail with little or no experience. About 15% had absolutely no previous experience and another 15% had less than a year. The smell of the woods and a yearning for adventure is all that some women need to set the soul stirring and the imagination dreaming of the white blazes.

"I thru-hiked the Trail without any backpacking experience" recalls Nancy Marth, Geo. "I simply had the desire, determination, and perseverance to succeed. You need to have a strong will to want to do a thru-hike. The physical part is important but the Trail gets you in shape; it's the mental part that keeps you going."

Joyce Johnson, Pilgrim's Progress, met thru-hikers ranging in age from 13 to 87. "They all had the enthusiasm, physical strength and inner strength that it takes." Joyce feels you need to have a general knowledge of the out-of-doors, a few safety and survival skills, but most of all the deep down desire to want to hike.

Two-time thru-hiker, Susan Roquemore, Dragon Lady, says "Old enough to walk at least. Experience enough to not be afraid of the dark and

1

of creepy crawlies. Maturity in outlook with a healthy sense of humor is vital." Anne Mausolff, The Green Mountaineer, adds personal inner strengths and determination. Donna Horn warns that serious couch potatoes may have a tough time.

"The key to a successful thru-hike is a person's mind," according to Sue Freeman, Blueberry. "It takes commitment, perseverance, goal orientation, and flexibility. I watched women succeed in age from teens to well into their 70's. Age had no bearing on strength, endurance, physical fitness, speed, or attitude. Likewise, women with little or no experience fared just as well as their experienced counterparts."

When Carey Field, Pennsylvania Rose, hit the Trail in 1990 she was 18 with little hiking and no backpacking experience. "I'd always loved the outdoors and was very active in caving, whitewater rafting, canoeing, and just being out in nature when I was in high school. But I didn't know anyone who backpacked. Before I left, I read everything I could get my hands on, bought my equipment (mostly inexpensive stuff-all I could afford), and left with a spirit of adventure. Although I didn't finish the Trail, I had the best experience of my life and I'm going back someday soon."

At 19, Carolyn Cunningham, Tawanda, began her thru-hike having very little life experience in terms of being independent and making major decisions on her own. "I believe anyone can do a thru-hike at any point in their lives as long as they have the will power and dedication. The Trail taught me to be mistress of my own destiny and take control of the things I wanted to do. I did have a lot of backpacking experience through Outward Bound and working at an outdoor education center. But, I also ran into many people, both male and female, who had never hiked in their lives. I found these people to be the most inspiring because they were forced to be flexible and learn by doing. Sometimes their learning came in the form of failing miserably. But when I saw them learning from their mistakes and making it to Katahdin or their destination, I became aware that hiking the Trail is not about doing everything 'right' but doing it the way each person pleases."

Women & Thru-Hiking on the Appalachian Trail

Kay Cutshall, The Old Gray Goose, was 53 when she began hiking the Trail in two big sections in '92-'93. She is married, the mother of three, and grandmother of ten. "I had no backpacking experience, camping, yes...hiking, no! I first read in a '91 AARP bulletin article about the AT and a woman who was a year older than I who had hiked the Trail. The more I read about it, the more interested I became. Finally my husband said, 'Well, when are you going to do it?' I joined the Appalachian Trail Conference on my birthday, October 30, and started planning for a spring start. After 2 1/2 months hiking I found out what homesickness was all about and went home to regroup. I started out the next year at about the same place I got off and about the same time so I would at least feel like I was thru-hiking. I had family support and although my husband is unable to hike, he fully supports me on my hiking adventures."

Since 1979 Nellie Hayse has been making an annual pilgrimage to the Trail completing 500 miles alone but often hikes in the company of a small group of friends. She has logged over 1500 miles and hopes to become a 2000 miler within the next five years. At 62 Nellie loves being on the Trail. No fear. No serious problems. Wonderful experiences. A lifetime of fun and memories.

"An obsessive drive to hike the Trail is number one," emphasizes Lisa Barter, Tinkerbell. "It certainly takes self-confidence, an ability to combine planning skills and fly by the seat of your pants openness, a vision, and a goal. I would never have finished the Trail without a certain amount of grit my teeth stick-to-it-tive-ness. There are days when it's just wretched to be out there. The ability to enjoy the present moment and also see beyond it is essential. I am reluctant to set any sort of age limitation other than a woman should be at least 18 considering the high incidence of party situations and tavern visits; 21 is even better. Mostly, it's when you can say to yourself that you are doing this because it is of utmost importance to you, not just because you're trying to escape something. If you can still walk and don't have any prohibitive health problems, it's never too late."

Cleo Wolf, Footloose, feels all it takes is persistence. "I learned while hiking Springer to Baxter that hiking is 99% mental and 1% anything else. It is will and determination that keeps putting one foot in front of the other. Sometimes I had to count each step. I'd count to thirteen and start over again, and gradually I began to love flying down or up the Trail. It was no longer uncomfortable after the first few minutes in the morning while my feet complained. I felt like a deer or a bird, I was strong and at home. Dogged determination; that's the qualification you need."

Kelly Winters, Amazin' Grace, thru-hiked in '96 and thinks a sense of humor, willingness to endure extreme discomfort for a long time, and an open mind can come in handy. "Being comfortable and at ease in the woods can sure help, but if a woman isn't, she'll sure learn in a hurry or leave the Trail. It's not a nice walk in the woods. It's very hard, but if you know that, it won't bother you."

Section hiking over several years, Gail Mary Francis, gmf, drew on her high school athletic experience. "During the first week or so I can remember carrying a pack that was insanely heavy with too much stuff and trying to make my way up the mountains. I would feel like I just couldn't possibly go another step, but then I'd go for a few more miles. My experience running cross country in high school was useful to get my mind whipped into shape in terms of what limitations I would and wouldn't accept from my body. As a former runner, I had similar feelings, but I knew that a second wind would come along as long as I didn't cave into the immediate weariness."

In leading and instructing workshops on long distance hiking Melody Blaney, Midnite, '96, tells women that age doesn't matter and that anyone can physically hike the AT. "But, you mentally have to put up with endless days of rain, bugs, and pain. Prior experience in backpacking helps, but the Trail will teach you everything you need to know for the novice. The only limitations are the ones we place on ourselves."

Communication: Support from Family and Friends

Effectively communicating the Trail experience to loved ones has significance at various stages of preparing and hiking the Trail. Just as the prospective thru-hiker immerses herself in information on the Trail, she will find that sharing her preparation with friends and family involves them

4

in the adventure and helps them to understand the breadth and depth of the experience. Family and friends help prepare and send supplies/maildrops to designated post offices on or near the Trail, may meet and hike with the hiking family member, or write letters and post cards. The hiker, in return, writes frequently, calls whenever possible from a phone near the Trail, and more recently e-mails from locations near the Trail having computer internet access.

The survey asked hikers if they received support from family and friends. Although many reported that loved ones "just didn't understand," usually someone in their lives did support their plans for a thru-hike. Occasionally there was opposition in the family, in several cases the father, which was balanced by another supportive member, the mother. Rarely did a woman report that she received only opposition to her thru-hiking plans.

Bravery can take many forms. "When I made my decision to thru-hike I had no idea the impact my decision to hike the Trail would have on my life. The decision to leave my husband for six months to hike the Trail was not something done by a woman in my conservative Baptist circle. Women are supposed to be 'keepers at home.' But my decision to hike brought righteous indignation not just toward me, but also toward my husband. He was made to feel guilty because he was supporting me on the Trail. At one point while I was on the Trail the 'friends' in our church told him he ought to insist that I come off the Trail and come home. I see how difficult it was for him to keep upbeat with his support while I was hiking. My decision to hike the Trail involved him more than I realized at the time."

Suzanne Konopka, Doc, writes, "You cannot 'convince' anyone you will be safe anymore than you can guarantee it for yourself. Anything can happen. People will worry the way they usually do. My father thought I'd get killed out there because he has always been overcautious, to put it mildly. He stayed depressed the whole time I was hiking. My mom and sister were thrilled for me, and they were my best supporters. Sure, they probably worried some, but normally so." Sue also adds that there are few major emergencies on the AT and does not agree with cell phones and other "techno-polluting" trash in the wilderness.

Women & Thru-Hiking on the Appalachian Trail

Sue Kenn, White Glove, thinks it's impossible to convince loved ones that you will be safe on a thru-hike. "You can only assure them that you will be as cautious and careful as possible and that you'll use common sense. During my first thru-hike my mom was always sending me newspaper clippings telling me about accidents and rapes on hiking trails. She told me to always be aware of who is behind and who is ahead of me."

A young woman writes, "I started my hike in March and my father was terrified of his little girl being out in the woods all alone. Someone at his company sent him the two-part PBS Trailside tape about thru-hiking hoping it would give him some perspective. It really helped him to understand what I was doing out there. I watched it when I got home and cried and cried at the part where the young man goes home because of a stress fracture, which is why I am sitting here writing now instead of hiking somewhere in New York state."

When it became apparent that she could not convince certain loved ones that she would be safe on the Trail, section-hiker Diane Kortan focused on trying to demonstrate that she was sensitive to their concerns by preparing a detailed itinerary of her anticipated day-to-day progress. "From information supplied in the Trail Guides, I was able to list the shelter where I expected to spend the night along with the name, address, and telephone number of the ranger station with jurisdiction over that section of the Trail. I told them I would be sure to sign the register at each shelter so that I could be easily traced. Most importantly, I was able to indicate on the list when and where I would have access to a telephone and would be calling home. It was reassuring to them to know that if I failed to call within a day or two of an expected time, they had at hand the phone number of a ranger station to initiate an inquiry."

Regina Erskine, Whispering Pine, found carrying a pre-paid phone card convenient. "I also wrote down 1-800 numbers of my friends and family so that I could keep in touch for free. In each town I would send out a bunch of postcards and call my 'contact' person at home so that at least one person was posted on my whereabouts."

Kelly Winters, Amazin' Grace, suggests giving loved ones lots of information and material that shows you've done a lot of planning. "Give them a copy of Wingfoot's handbook and let them follow along as you walk. I would call home from a town and say, 'Hi Mom, I'm in Podunkville, it's on page 64.' And she'd say, 'Oh, are you at that hostel with the all-you-can-eat breakfast? That sounds nice.' Otherwise, they have this vision of you just being out there somewhere in the woods, unreachably remote."

"My mother, who likes tangible evidence, was reassured by my maildrop schedule, food lists, books on the Trail, etc. Also, the further I hiked, the more she realized that I did know what I was doing out there, that I was perfectly capable, that there were other hikers around, and that I really would call her from towns. It will take time if you feel you need to convince your loved ones. If you can, take them to a Trail town, hostel, or other contact point so they can get a feel for the kind of life you'll be having, and let them talk to other people who have hiked, or to their loved ones."

Joyce Johnson, Pilgrim's Progress, received prayer-o-grams from the pastor of her church and posted her maildrop schedule on the church bulletin board. Many hikers also find a great deal of support from outside their immediate family and circle of friends. In recent years, hikers have written on-line journals. A friend at home transcribes their letters for others to read and sends on encouragement from those following the hiker's journey.

"Call home as often as you can," suggests Sarah Dixon. "I was surprised at how many opportunities the Trail yielded. When you least expected it, there would be a little store-ice cream, soda, and a phone call home! I wrote only in my journal and made tapes. I had a little cassette recorder that I would talk to at all different times. I sent tapes home, and then the family would pass them around. That was easier since I was so tired at the end of the day and just barely had the energy to write in my journal. The tapes were always more interesting anyway."

For hikers too weary to write those all so important journals, ask friends and family to save all the cards and letters sent home. If you write them noting the mileage and date on each and focus on some interesting content, they can serve as a type of journal. Chronicling the AT adventure is extremely significant for most thru-hikers and this can take a variety of forms from journaling and sketching, photos and slides, to saving memorabilia. Gail Johnson, Gutsy, firmly believes that these activities "keep the hike alive," helping you to savor the memories of your months on the Trail.

Gutsy also adds, "I have decided that hiking the AT is a very selfish thing to do, and I feel badly sometimes for the worry I caused my family while I was on the Trail (not to mention that they had to fend for themselves). I was in the Shenandoahs in '96 when two women were murdered. I did offer to come home at that point because I didn't want to make my husband's life miserable with worry. But all in all, I'm glad I did it and the gains from my thru-hike were great for me. The good was passed on to my family in the way of a more relaxed me. I learned on the Trail how to separate what is really important from what really doesn't matter and my entire family benefits from that."

Some hikers send articles to their local newspapers or connect with a local school or community group. Beverly Hugo, Maine Rose, did pre-hike and post-hike presentations for a second grade class and a group of senior citizens all over age 70 at her local Jewish Community Center. Both groups received a map of the AT mounted on foam board along with a maildrop list to keep in touch. As Rosie's cards and letters came in, they were read aloud and tacked on the maps. Everyone learned a lot about geography and vicariously enjoyed the adventure as she progressed north. Rosie also used her educational background to develop a unique Maine Studies/Appalachian Trail curriculum that incorporates a hands-on approach adaptable for multiple grade levels.

Carolyn Thalman is a women's on-line list member and special education teacher. She encourages thru-hikers to write to her students and has observed remarkable progress due to the high interest and excitement generated by following the hikers on their journey north.

"AT Gracie"-Trail Angel

Former hikers and friends of the Trail, often called Trail Angels, support the crop of current thru-hikers in any given year through writing letters and providing acts of loving-kindness. When this is spontaneous, such as a convenient lift to town or a piece of fresh fruit given by a day hiker, it is a real joy to receive. Too much abundance of trail magic, however, can contaminate the thru-hiker's experience.

Tammy Richards, AT Gracie, is a real friend of many thru-hikers some she has met in person and some only through correspondence.

My experience as a Trail Angel began several years ago. I remember seeing the trailhead on Route 4 near Rangeley, Maine and became fascinated with this path through the woods that someone called the Appalachian Trail. I knew nothing about the Trail at the time but was immediately drawn to it, wondering where it began and where it might lead. Little did I know that the Trail would become a big part of my life.

It seems right that I have fallen in love with the Trail and have a deep respect for those who undertake the inward journey to walk its length of over 2,000 miles. As a small child, I would plead with my parents to take me to the mountains where I felt I belonged, knowing that just seeing the mountains for a day would fill a place deep inside that craved to be at one with the wild places. When I learned the story behind the Appalachian Trail, I felt I had come home.

What a commitment to decide to walk the entire 2,000 plus miles, with each day spent living the Trail and experiencing the forests and mountains! Even having the opportunity to visit the towns it passes strikes me as a special part of hiking the Trail. The Trail is made up of people, those who call the mountains home and the hikers who are often changed by this dream they have felt a need to fulfill. Those people are also a reason I love the Trail so much.

Since I am a single mom who dreams of a thru-hike, but do not feel I could leave my son for an extended period of time right now, I have opted to experience the Trail in another way. I have become Gracie the Trail Angel and work hard to be an asset in the life of the Trail. While there is some controversy regarding the work of trail angels and just how much is too much, I must say I strive to become a positive part of the hikers' overall experience. I send cards, letters, and even goodie packages to those hikers

I meet prior to or during their hikes, but make every effort not to hone in on their experiences on the Trail and do not make a pest of myself. I believe in my own dream to thru-hike the Trail someday. Realizing the hike will be more heart than head, as Grandma Gatewood said, I hope my efforts via the postal service will be enough to provide needed encouragement to a weary hiker. A card arriving at a time when it is most needed can gently remind the hiker of the motivation that got him/her to the northern or southern terminus of this wondrous trail in the first place and of the inner strength behind that very first of five million steps that moved them forward on the Appalachian Trail.

Mitch's story- A family's support

Barbara and Steve Landis, parents of 20 year old Michele, (Mitch), planned on driving their daughter twelve hours to the Springer Mountain trailhead. Mitch had researched her hike for two years, done aerobics and weight training to get in shape, and talked with dozens of thru-hikers at her job at a store servicing the hiking community. Barbara had pledged logistical support but wasn't entirely happy with her daughter starting out without a partner. Steve had backpacked and hitchhiked across the country when he was 21 and felt it only fitting that Mitch use the same carved walking stick he had used on his adventure so many years before. They stopped in Virginia and attended Palm Sunday Eve mass. Mitch couldn't stop weeping from stress and anxiety, complained of nausea, and left the service in tears. She told her parents she couldn't go through with it and tearfully apologized for making them drive all the way down there just to have to turn around and go back home.

　　Barbara was disappointed and relieved at the same time. "Instead of trying to placate her or rescue her, I focused entirely on making her comfortable in the car while her father handled the situation calmly and rationally. He suggested we continue southward since we had already reserved a room for the night in the beautiful Amicolola Falls Lodge and we'd been looking forward to staying there. So we traveled on with our daughter stretched out in the back seat, barely able to move, her stomach was so upset. She slept. She slept through our supper stop, through a bathroom stop, and through the late-night drive in the Black Mountains of the Smokies where I imagined her sleeping alone deep in those dark woods. I cried quietly to myself, as I am now, remembering my anxiety. Many hours later we reached the lodge. She ran ahead into the building and disappeared emerging later weak, pale, and exhausted. She had vomited in the lobby's bathroom toilet along with the fear she had carried for so long. As soon as she hit the bed, she slept a deep and restful sleep, and by morning, she was good to go."

Sitting on the swinging chair on Wingfoot's porch during Trailfest, the author chatted with two hikers, one a young, confident, exuberant woman who had just completed 270 miles of the Trail and was having the time of her life. Mitch was bright, happy, and cheerful as she recounted her story of pre-hike fear and anxiety and the conversation ended with a parting hug.

Mitch's parents joined the Trailplace website listserve so her ongoing progress was noted on the list. Returning to Maine from Hot Springs in the summer after writing most of this book, the author had the opportunity to have breakfast with Barbara and Steve at their home and check out Mitch's photos of the 1500 miles she had already traveled on her way north to Katahdin. Mitch's grandparent's contribution to her hike was a donation of single use cameras so Mitch could send them home for speedy developing and keeping her family abreast of her travels and adventures. Another daughter, Stephanie, is planning her own thru-hike and the whole family, including an older brother, has joined Mitch on the Trail for short sections. Barbara and Steve have maps of the Trail at work so many friends have a regular update of Mitch's progress. The love and support of family can be crucial to a hiker's successful thru-hike.

Both Barb and Steve notified the listserves when Mitch summited Katahdin on October 14. Steve wrote. "It was a Class 2 day with lots of ice and poor visibility. Her platypus drinking tube froze on the way up. The sign at the top was iced over. She is awesome." Barb wrote. "Conditions were Class 2, meaning hiking not recommended. Mitch said she was in a cloud the entire 5.2 miles to the summit. The first four miles were very difficult due to the ice-covered boulders requiring foot-grabbing maneuvers. The last mile was flat and easy. She and her friends took each other's pictures at the ice-covered sign marking the end of the Trail. Beards were frozen, hands were numb, but they made it!"

"We have four photo albums and a huge scrapbook of letters, postcards, and telephone logs. The adventure that began April 5 from Springer Mt in Georgia has taken her through rain, hail, sleet and snow. We can't wait to see her and listen to her stories. She has tales of bear, moose, Canadian jays…even porcupines. I am so amazed that she has really done this. How many times I have heard her say in the last few months, 'Mom, it's no big deal…I'm just walking from Georgia to Maine. Lots of people do it.'"

How can you justify leaving children and loved ones?

It is not usual to see either men or women thru-hiking the Trail and leaving school age children at home with a partner or other family members. There may be not only tremendous guilt in leaving family behind but also the extra-added stress for the partner at home. However, while it is not frowned upon by the men on the Trail to see a dad thru-hiking, a woman may incur severe criticism and has a whole different set of issues before she is ready to leave a child or children behind. In certain circumstances unique to each individual woman and her family, some women have managed successfully to thru-hike often to the benefit of all concerned.

On her return, Joyce Johnson, Pilgrim's Progress, had to justify this to some of her neighbors more than she did her husband or family. "My husband, kids, and I discussed my hike in great depth. The daughters were grown and away from home. My oldest son was 18, still living at home but working two jobs so he could afford to get married. My youngest son was 10 and I had to consider his care in my absence. My husband said, 'You have been here for 28 years, raising my children, working only at home, helping me with our business, doing whatever needed to be done, when it needed to be done. This is definitely not what I would want to do, but if this is what you want to do, go do it. I know that you can!' My 10 year old said,

'It is a cool idea, and Dad will take care of me'."

Although many women thru-hikers have more than 10 years of backpacking experience before they start their hikes, many also have little or no experience and manage quite successfully. Beverly Hugo, Maine Rose '95, is a single mom who had two days' backpacking experience when she solo thru-hiked the Trail at age 48. "The first person I contacted after making the decision to thru-hike was my ex-husband living in Trinidad, West Indies. He readily agreed that our son would be taken out of the 6th grade at the beginning of March and enrolled in an international school on the island for the remainder of the school year. Our daughter was to finish the remainder of her freshman year of high school under the supervision of two of my sisters who shared our family childhood home. She would then spend the summer in Trinidad with her father."

"I thought I would finish in six months like all the books suggested. I didn't. It took me seven months, averaging 10 miles a day. A third sister came from Michigan to help get the kids ready for school. Thank you Candy, Ruth-Anne, and Janice! I only saw my children for a half day in that period and started to miss them terribly once they had returned to Maine and I was hiking on the last leg of the AT in my home state. I feel I left a personal legacy of self-reliance and independence to both my children that I hope they will emulate. My daughter, Saretta, graduated from high school at 17 and deferred college enrollment. A week after graduation she was on a plane, alone, and spent the next year in a self-designed individualized program working, traveling, and studying in Australia, New Zealand, Spain, and England. A thru-hike can influence our loved ones in ways we can only imagine."

Avid section hiker Barbara DiGiovanni, D-Boss, writes, "When my children were little I didn't hike because they needed me. When my parents were sick I didn't hike because they needed me. Now my parents are dead and my children are grown. I have hiking time because I teach and vacations are long enough to do some serious mileage. I don't regret not hiking but I sure wish I had. It would have given me the opportunity to separate myself from the pressures of caring for needy people. I did not take enough time for myself, and that I do regret. One cannot always

13

choose to do what one wants all the time, but you must make time for yourself. Having cared for many aged people in my family, I must say dropping dead on the Trail is sure better than Alzheimers or heart failure. I, for one, am going to hike till I drop if I have a chance."

Cheryl Gaudreau, Soulmates, thru-hiked in '98 leaving her 17 year old daughter who was just about to have her birthday. "This was the first birthday I ever missed and boy, did I feel guilty. We had never been apart for more than four days in a row and now we were separated for four months. She came out to hike with me for five days and we again parted with a tearful goodbye. We both survived, however. My daughter encouraged me to do this thru-hike with Ron, my new husband. She reminded me that all my life I had done without and made sacrifices so that she could have a good life. She informed me that it was time that I did something for myself. She told me it was time 'to be selfish' and follow my heart, pursue my dreams, and that I had better 'chill out' real soon!"

"My daughter became my biggest fan and the best moral support person you could ever ask for. She moved in with her paternal grandparents and still resides with them. My ex-husband rudely informed me when I returned home that I had made HIS life miserable while I was away. He got to learn what raising a teenager is all about. I did it without his help for 16 years and he panicked over six months and he had his parents to assist him. My daughter never once complained that her mom was 1,000 miles away, and we still had our long talks. I spent a fortune on calling cards."

"I had many worries while I was away, but they lessened with each phone call home. My daughter 'turned her life around.' She has become incredibly independent, decided to make an effort in school for the first time in her life, has taken control of her life, and has matured into a wonderful young lady who I am very proud of. She has since remarked that my thru-hike was the best thing that ever happened to both of us."

Cheryl cautions hikers that their children will be different when they return from thru-hiking. "They will change and so will you. The current relationship won't be the same, but it may be better." Cheryl does state that she would not have left her daughter under the age of 15 because she was raising her alone. "If she had been younger and had I still been married to her dad, I wouldn't have thought twice about going. I would have gone in a heartbeat. Men are very capable of raising their children while their partner is away for a length of time. It may be the best way to build a strong relationship."

Lisa Barter, Tinkerbell, describes an "a-ha!" experience gleaned from her thru-hike. "I had innumerable day and weekend hikers tell me that they were envious and wished that they could hike the Trail. After pondering this for a while, I realized that all the folks out there thru-hiking made some serious sacrifices and choices. Realizing a hike is a choice that must be made, and while there are some conditions in our lives that are more conducive to a hike than others (being single, not having dependents, and being at a transition point in a career), there is always a window of opportunity. We just have to be willing to make the sacrifices and go for it."

Growing up, section hiker Marcia Fairweather, Almost There, heard three sayings from older folks more than enough times. "If only I knew then what I know now," "I regret doing such and such," and "I sacrificed everything for my family and have gotten nothing in return." "These words have echoed in my mind each time I have come to a cross-road or major decision that could impact others or promote or limit me in some way. This has driven me to feel that I must enjoy this life. I must do and be all that my heart desires, and I will never say these words if I can help it. So the choice to leave the dependents and family behind when nature or my instinct calls becomes an obvious choice for me-to go! I am married with a six year old at this time, and there have been many occasions where I had to choose the action that benefits me the most."

Christine is a single mom planning a '99 thru-hike. "I have an eight year old daughter. She is a strong independent young girl who I believe can handle the six month separation. I guess I'm lucky that I have a mother who has a large house and the means to take on raising a child for six months so I can go off and pursue my dream. I think really the word dream is the keyword here. I am doing this thru-hike because it is a dream of mine, but I also believe by doing so it will help my daughter realize that dreams can be pursued and reached."

15

"My mother and I discussed what would be the best way to handle Torrie in my preparations and we decided that first it would be important for her to get settled in a new environment and establish a routine. We moved in with my mother approximately nine months prior to my departure date. My mother has a large house with a few rooms to choose from. We told Torrie to select a room of her own. She did and we decorated it to her specifications…pink walls, purple ceilings with over 500 stars and curtains and bedspread to match. There is a little guilt that goes along with leaving a child so I may have over compensated in this area. She now has a room worthy of a decorator magazine."

"I also thought it was important to point out on a fairly regular basis how things will be different when I'm on the Trail. I drive her to school every morning and while she lives with my mother she will go to school on the bus. House rules will also change. She has time to get used to these with my reinforcement so they don't seem so extreme. As time has progressed and I started doing my food preparation, I let her get involved. She is my spaghetti leather roller and she samples all of the dried vegetables before they go into a bag. I also took her to the ALDHA Gathering (the annual meeting of the Appalachian Long Distance Hikers Association-www.aldha.org), to meet and experience some trail people and sit through a talk on food drying. It amazes me everyday how we will be in a store and she will spot something and ask me if this is something I would like sent to me. She has vowed to bake me brownies and 100 mile wilderness bread from a recipe she found in the Logue's AT coloring book. I have set aside enough air-fare for 2 visits for her to meet me on the Trail if she needs to see me although I'm hoping this won't be necessary. I will get her a Mizpah necklace and give it to her before we part. She'll wear one half and I the other."

"I have seen this child grow more mature in only the anticipation of the Trail and I look forward to seeing how she is after the Trail. She is currently a straight A student who is in an accelerated learning program at her school. I had a conference with her teacher and let her know when I would be leaving and that if she saw any changes that were hurting Torrie's school work to let my mother know."

16

Women & Thru-Hiking on the Appalachian Trail

A woman contemplating a thru-hike expresses powerful sentiments felt by many women.

Sometimes I have wondered if I have spent most of my life in wonder and guilt about doing the right thing. If I do what is right for me and what will make me happy and others don't agree, will they still love me? Will they still be there for me when I get back? I suppose it makes family members uncomfortable to see good old Mom venturing out, trying something new, doing something that she didn't get permission to do; something that is just for her and not for anyone else. Society drums it in our heads over and over that women need to take care of others and that people are depending on us, to put aside our needs for the good of the family. Whether we like it or not, we get sucked up into the pitch before we even know it, and then we finally realize, hey, I have a life, too. I want to do some things that don't involve the family. We leave behind our loved ones and we will miss them and they will miss us. When you think about it, it is only a very short period of time out of our entire lives that we will be gone on our journey. Talk to someone about regrets and you will never hear anyone say they regret getting a good education, or that they regret learning to play a musical instrument, or that they regret hiking the Appalachian Trail. The only regrets heard were those not attempted.

The teen-age daughter of a thru-hiker writes to her mother in the midst of her own solo adventure abroad. "I wanted to write you today because I am feeling especially grateful-grateful for having you. This year wouldn't have been possible without your guidance, support, and love. I know it sounds incredibly mushy, but there is no other way to say it. You are more than a mother-if someone can be more than this. You have helped me in every possible way and your voice has been a real comfort this year and throughout my whole life. There have been many times when I have been almost out of money or hope, or just overcome by a feeling of helplessness and your words of encouragement pushed me to get things done. I feel like I can't make it up to you- I want to have your strength and courage. I want your adventurous spirit. I want your kind heart and your motivation. And now I am crying because I miss you so much. Or rather I am feeling such great pride for you and I didn't think it was possible. I

don't think I could ever thank you enough for what you have given me."
Mothers and women who mother....take risks and be brave for our
daughters. Let us model by example and in turn grow ourselves.

Preparation

*"If you are ready to leave father and mother, and brother and sister, and
wife and child and friends, and never see them again,--if you have paid
your debts, and made your will, and settled all your affairs, and are a free
man, then you are ready for a walk."*

Henry David Thoreau

Thoreau would undoubtedly have included "free women" if he had
known about women thru-hikers especially those who wisely hit the Trail
with all their home obligations handled responsibly and efficiently. Like
many things on the Trail there are multiple ways to get the job done. There
may be a preferred way or a safer way or a recommended way but usually
not the only way. Some hikers mistakenly believe that the formula for a
successful thru-hike includes the "perfect" most sophisticated hi-tech gear,
the most detailed maildrop schedule, the most ultra-light of everything with
caloric requirements worked out for every meal and snack. Hikers often
feel more secure taking courses in basic first aid, CPR, and map and
compass reading. However, others just follow the white blazes and fit their
first aid kit into a sandwich bag. A flexible outlook, adaptable attitude,
perseverance, and tenacity are not taught in any book or course. They also
don't add packweight.

Leslie Croot, '94, prepared herself mentally by reading. "Every
'negative' thing that happened, I had read about and expected. When they
occurred, I didn't feel demoralized. I felt normal! My response was, 'Hey,
I read about this, this is ok. Overcoming this is what will make me
stronger.' And it did."

A '98 hiker is a firm believer that anything from running a mile to
hiking 2000 miles is 95% mental and 5% physical. "I got in decent shape
before my thru-hike just through lifting weights, running, skiing, and

18

snowboarding. I was in nowhere near the shape of most of the other people I encountered, but after a few weeks I was easily hiking a decent distance each day. More than anything I did previous to my hike, I just mentally pushed on and the Trail got me in shape."

Beverly Hugo, Maine Rose, had never heard of thru-hiking until June 1994. "I immersed myself totally in the Trail reading everything, watching videos time and time again, and attending three AT presentations, two at L.L. Bean. By that time I had chosen my Trailname, Maine Rose. A panel member and power hiker said I couldn't do that and had to 'find one' on the Trail as had been previous tradition. Too late! I already had calling cards printed up to give to hikers along the way."

Do yourself a favor and stay away from negative people. You do not have to justify your hike to anyone but yourself and the immediate loved ones who may be directly affected by your absence. A woman who is overweight and not in shape need not subject herself to the criticism that is likely to come her way in the form of derisive side glance looks or belittling remarks by people who have no idea what is in your heart and soul. If necessary, despite your eagerness to share your upcoming adventure, either keep it to yourself or within the confines of a supportive group, on or off-line.

Maine Rose adds, "Treating a woman hiker to a meal and picking her brain is another excellent method of getting first hand information. Joyce Mailman, Espy, of '94 hardly had a chance to eat her Indian food for all the questions my sister, as my support team, and I asked her." Espy was written up in her local newspaper and has a tradition, along with her twin sister, of hiking Mt. Washington ...on New Year's Eve!

"I also got a lot of information on-line and e-mailed hikers before Wingfoot's website became active. My living room was turned into operations central with a big map of the AT on the wall and a foam board covered with visual reminders of the hike: maildrop list, cards from well wishers, the AT symbol, packaging from gorp fixins, and a gear list that always seemed to be refined and revised on a daily basis."

A voracious reading habit seems to afflict women when planning a thru-hike. Joining the ATC, Appalachian Trail Conference, is often the first step in the process of gaining important information about the Trail. This resource gathering process can be a critical part of a woman's successful hike. She may steep herself in AT lore amassing detailed information about gear, recipes, hygiene, and safety, visiting countless outfitters, watching videos, spending months or years on listserves, and having an ear always tuned to any mention of the Appalachian Trail.

Women's thorough detailed planning seems to be especially significant in building confidence and easing anxiety and pre-hike stress if that is an issue. As indicated by the survey, over 25% of women 2000 milers planned their thru-hikes for over a year. Many of these women already had more than five years and sometimes ten years of hiking and backpacking experience.

While the Trail has been a part of many women's lives for a number of years, others can pinpoint the exact time and place when they first realized that this 2,160-mile footpath is available for them to hike. The trigger might be a book, a TV show, a newspaper article, a community talk, a video, an interview, a seminar, or a passing remark by another hiker while walking in the woods. Something clicks inside. It can even remain dormant and fester. The occasional woman may harbor resentment because she feels tied to responsibilities and can't take the time to thru-hike. The flash that lights in women's minds may be a call to action. So pay attention. It can be daunting and intimidating at the beginning stages of a new challenge. It is also an opportunity to be passionate about a new project. In preparing for a thru-hike, every training step adds to your knowledge and thus your confidence to undertake this new adventure.

However, it is also critical while on the Trail to be able to adapt to changing plans and any glitch that may occur. One hiker, after numerous schedule adjustments lamented that schedules are good for two things, toilet paper and fire starters. Beverly Hugo, Maine Rose, spent months planning maildrops and working on a schedule. "It didn't take long for me to realize that I would be behind my original plan. I even stopped cooking in Tennessee eating cold food on the Trail most of the time and hot meals in towns. I instructed my sister to hold the dehydrated food. There's a plastic container with Ziplocs filled with dehydrated beans still taking up space in the pantry years after my thru-hike. If I would ever thru-hike again, I wouldn't even bother with drops at all and just buy groceries along the way."

Although some women managed to secure a leave of absence or sabbatical from their jobs, a greater percentage of women thru-hikers simply quit. Others work seasonally to allow themselves to hike when they prefer and several are retired. They are risk takers willing to take a chance to experience the adventure of the AT.

Young women still living at home with their parents greatly reduce their personal expenses. More than one hiker has put all her things in storage and given up an apartment not knowing if she would be injured or off the Trail within a week. Hikers pay bills ahead of time, get their taxes done early, and make sure a friend or family member handles the homefront, feeds the cat, and waters the plants. Women leave their loved ones including children. They make new wills, take out insurance, pay their debts, and arrange for power of attorney with someone they trust. They join gyms, set up their own individualized exercise programs, and enlist others in their vision. The time is right. Some women feel it in their core and thru-hiking is a dramatic expression of that self-affirmation.

Kelly Winters, Amazin' Grace, trained for the Trail by running, walking, and hiking around downtown Washington, D.C. with a fully-loaded pack. "People thought I was homeless. I commuted to work by walking with the pack. People at work thought I was loony, but who cared? I was leaving soon anyway. At lunchtime, I'd go up and down the stairs in the office buildings where I was temping wearing my pack. I also went into the subway and ran up the down escalator. You can train anywhere."

Sue Kenn, White Glove, was an avid day hiker often hitting the Trail with her dad when they first started discussing thru-hiking. To see if they could handle the AT, their preparation was a thru-hike of the 268-mile Long Trail.

The Long Trail, running the length of Vermont from Massachusetts to the Canadian border, shares its southern one hundred miles with the AT. Hikers who have ventured on the section north of the Inn at Long Trail would heartily agree that this section is a challenge indeed. Like Sue and her dad, Ted Bartlett, Poledragger, many hikers gain confidence from weekend backpacking trips. Longer excursions lasting up to a couple of weeks help them determine if they can handle the extended period of time in the outdoors. Women thru-hikers frequently recommended these "shakedown" hikes of various lengths to gauge food needs and preferred hiking speeds, and learn how to handle the elements.

"I was very naive about the AT. We stood on Springer in front of the mail box and couldn't believe that a postman came all the way up there to collect mail. Is it possible? Not feeling quite sure about it, we put a note with our postcards asking someone to send them out for us if they were still there in a few days. Someone did and they arrived home shortly afterwards." The "mailbox" is a metal drawer imbedded in a rock and holds the Trail register. These Trail registers, usually spiral bound notebooks kept in large Ziploc bags, are found in every shelter. On their '89 thru-hike this father-daughter team, self-described as both having a lot of patience, celebrated their birthdays; Sue turned 37 and Ted, 68.

While in the White Mountains a day hiker approached Sue and asked her if she was a thru-hiker. He had never met one and was curious about the adventure she was having with her father. So eight years later, Sue and new husband Dick, the curious day hiker, prepared for a '98 thru-hike. How? By again thru-hiking the Long Trail with Sue's dad along for the fun!

Sue describes the thru-hike with her dad as a "quiet" hike while the one with Dick, Duster, a more social experience. "Having already done the Trail, I know pretty much what to expect: cold, wet weather, hot days that don't seem to end, the fantastic Trail towns along the way, and the beautiful sections of Trail along with the not so beautiful. To be with my husband as he experiences the beauty of the Appalachian Trail will be yet another fantastic experience for me." Sue and Dick Kenn believe that by maintaining simplicity in their lives they can have time to enjoy each other and their time together.

Even experienced hikers, including those who have already thru-hiked, can get injured on the Trail. Sue Kenn writes of her '98 hike, "After 1,350 miles I developed plantar facsitis on my left foot. We were close to a road so I went to a clinic. After a shot of cortizone and a prescription for ibuprofen, the doctor told me I could probably continue. That problem no sooner cleared up than I stepped on a rock the wrong way and turned my ankle. My husband took some of the weight and I hobbled along. After almost a week, a very steep descent put the final touches on my already sore ankle. I decided it was time to get off the Trail. The pain prevented me from enjoying myself. Again, we were close to a road crossing." Dick later continued on and completed his thru-hike.

Lisa Barter, Tinkerbell, warns and rightfully so, "It is foolhardy to attempt a thru-hike without a moderate fitness level. Certainly, you will attain great fitness as you progress on your hike, but if you are not prepared, you will suffer tremendous aches and pains in your adjustment to the active lifestyle and greatly increase the chance of injury, perhaps permanent. I went into my '97 thru-hike fresh out of the mountains of Colorado. I'd already been extremely physically active and was used to backpacking, if only for a week at a time. I still had lots of stiff, sore muscle days and some excruciating knee pain at the start. Don't be lulled into thinking that you'll get in shape on the Trail. This amounts to the worst masochism imaginable. Instead, make sure that you have a moderate fitness level before starting."

How one achieves this moderate fitness level varies with the individual but always includes a lot of walking, with and without a pack. A weekly walk of 12-15 miles, in addition to a regular daily regimen, will give a woman some idea what it is like to stay on her feet for many hours at a time, a necessity for thru-hiking. Many women add short hiking and backpacking trips to their routines, jog, run, swim, do aerobics, and climb stairs with and without a pack. Those who feel comfortable at a gym start a weight routine focusing on the knees and legs, use the stairmaster or wear their packs on the treadmill putting it at increasing levels of elevation. Of the 2000 milers surveyed, 7% had no regular exercise program or did any physical preparation prior to their hike. It should be carefully noted that they were all between the ages of 20-29.

Ginny Owen, Spirit Walker, got ready for her two thru-hikes by walking and hiking. "Georgia has a lot of up and down. The first few weeks

23

were tough, but not as hard as they would have been if I hadn't been in good shape. I got tired and sore, but I was still happy out there, doing what I was doing. Those who start the Trail with the attitude that, 'I'll get in shape on the Trail,' have it much harder. Many of them don't last the first week. Those who do are pretty miserable."

Melody Blaney, Midnite, thinks that women tend to plan their hike more, i.e., maildrops, days off, nutritional needs, and may be a bit more rational in keeping mileage on an even level than male hikers. "Women consistently do average mileage days, rather than a string of high miles and then hang up in town for two days. Women seem to make the same progress with less hardships on our bodies and less chance of burning out."

Among the minority of hikers who are southbound, Emily Reith, Bugbite, started from Katahdin with two girlfriends. Temporarily laid up with a foot injury, she wanted to share her thoughts on mental toughness and backpacking prior to thru-hiking. "At the start the mental energy was spent convincing myself I really could do this and it would get easier. My partners and I had attended thru-hiking veteran Warren Doyle's workshop at The Gathering and found ourselves using some of his attitude phrases. 'At least they aren't wasps,' referring to the black flies and mosquitoes in Maine. 'At least the springs and streams aren't dry,' after four days of record breaking flooding. We even made up our own. At least we aren't on Mt. Everest, when we got hit by a hail and lightning storm while climbing Katahdin."

"I had done a fair amount of backpacking prior to the hike, but nothing could really prepare me for waking up each morning and knowing that I would be hiking today and again the next day for 180 some odd days. In the beginning that was really hard for me to get used to, but by the end of the 100-mile wilderness I had already become accustomed to my new life. It seemed normal and it was fun!" Emily, injury healed, returned to the Trail. Jackie, Emily's mom, notified the Trailplace listserves when Emily completed her south bound thru-hike on Springer.

Sawnie Robertson, Kinnickinic, has written a commitment to herself to help her focus on preparation for her thru-hike.

The single most important and determining piece of equipment I will take on the AT is my body. It is what will get me from place to place safely and in a timely manner. It cannot be replaced by another piece of like equipment that I hear will be more advantageous. It cannot be discarded as too heavy a burden. It must be just right, or suffer the consequences.

I and I alone can shape and mold this body, this vital piece of backpacking equipment. No one else can design or improve it. Only I can make it as lean as it needs to be or as strong as it will have to be. I cannot buy a replacement if it breaks down.

When I need to get over high rock or ledges, my body will have to be flexible enough to stretch where it needs to stretch. When I must get through small openings between large boulders, my body will have to be small enough to squeeze through.

My body begins its new year NOW... It will be sculpted and shaped and strengthened so that it will be a lean, healthy machine, ready to accomplish what is set before it... It will not be a hindrance. It will be an asset... because I am going to prepare it properly. I hope this sharing helps those of you who have expressed dismay over your present physical condition while planning to be in fit form for The Trail next year.

Gear

The process of researching gear, equipment, boots, and clothing for a thru-hike can involve extensive time, energy, and monetary resources. Most hikers, particularly if they are novices, must learn a whole new set of basic terms for this backpacking language. What is the difference between an internal and external frame pack? What are all these rests: therma, ridge, and z? What does it mean to sleep cold? What is the big deal anyway between cotton and all those other materials with fancy names: coolmax, polypro, supplex, capilene, and polartec? What are the advantages and disadvantages of a free standing vs. a staked tent? How do I choose a stove, and do I really want to cook anyway! There are so many decisions to make your mind spins.

Buying a few magazines such as Backpacker and Outside can be a starting point. The Backpacker Magazine annual gear issue is the single most comprehensive gear guide available and an excellent starting point. Visiting outfitters, pouring through catalogs, joining listserves, and researching on-line for a few months can help a woman become acquainted with the basic essentials necessary for a thru-hike. Although there are many on-line resources, they are in a constant state of flux and often promote specific lines rather than present an overall comprehensive assessment of all gear available, probably an impossible formidable task anyway.

It is easy to get caught up in the frenzy of making sure every little item is perfect. Sometimes the clothing in your drawers and the old stuff that has been around the basement or attic or garage for years can also fit the bill. Most hikers revise their supposed final gear list innumerable times before taking their first step on the Trail. Even then, many hikers send back a few too many pounds of unnecessary items at the 30-mile point at Neel's Gap sometimes continuing to pare down as they progress north. Hikers immerse themselves in gear talk for months before their hike. Interestingly enough, this continues for perhaps two weeks into a thru-hike at which time you have as much knowledge about equipment as you will probably ever need to hike the AT, and gear talk dramatically decreases.

More and more women are hitting the trails of America. With one out of three hikers a woman, manufacturers are taking into account a woman's body structure in gear design especially for packs, sleeping bags, boots, and clothing. Now if they would just ditch the fushia and other unnatural colors, we'd be a lot happier. Even with these innovations, however, many women often are quite satisfied with the traditional gear for men and find it serves their needs. This is, by no means, an exhaustive accounting of the myriad choices a woman has when purchasing gear. You will need to check out your local bookstore, outfitters, library, on-line resources, and magazine racks.

Don't forget when you enter the outfitter's that you are the consumer, the one with the credit card. Expect the salespeople to direct their attention to you and your needs and expect nothing less than the excellent attentive service you would expect to get in any other business establishment.

If you are lucky, you will have someone in your geographical area like Phil Somers and the backpacking department of L.L. Bean to advise you. Living within a half-hour drive of the retail store in Freeport, Maine made it easy for Beverly Hugo, Maine Rose, to make multiple visits before actually purchasing her first piece of gear. "On two occasions on pre-arranged visits, I took a full pack to the store at 7 a.m. meeting Phil by the scale in the camping department. He helped me get my pack weight down and gave me some wise suggestions for gear choices. He even sent me a few encouraging cards during my hike. We tried to connect near Grafton Notch but just missed each other. Phil and his wife, Darlene, had tacked a note up for me on a notice board giving me directions to a buried soda and an apple; thoughtful and appreciated simple Trail magic."

If you have received excellent service at your outfitters, write a letter and let the management know that the specified salesperson has taken special care of the needs of a thru-hiker. Find an outfitter that has a reasonable return policy and don't abuse it. What follows are a few brief gear considerations beneficial for women.

Packs

Try out a pack before purchasing or at least walk around the store with it loaded. An outfitter often has items to stuff into a pack making the fit more realistic although trying it out on the trail for a weekend may be more helpful. In an article from the June 1995 Backpacker, Kristin Hostetter discusses problems women have with a traditional pack fit.

Shoulder Harness: The harness is often too wide, causing the straps to slip sideways off women's narrower shoulders. This can sometimes be remedied by over-tightening the sternum strap, which in itself is uncomfortable. The unisex harness pads are typically too wide, too straight, and too long, causing chafing armpits and uncomfortable breast smashing.

Hipbelt: Often hipbelts don't match the flare of female hips, so the bottom edge digs in, while the top never touches the hips. Without a snug fit, chafing results and the woman inevitably loosens the hipbelt, which then doesn't perform its vital function of handling some of the pack's weight. The weight shifts to the shoulder harness which already fits poorly.

Torso Length: Women have a lower center of gravity, and generally feel more comfortable carrying the weight on their hips. If a pack's torso is too long, the hipbelt rides too low, and the shoulder straps bear the brunt of the load. Improper torso length also makes back and lumbar padding gap and bulge in the wrong places, which dooms all around comfort.

A future thru-hiker and woman diagnosed with attention deficit disorder has some special considerations in choosing a pack. "I've spoken with a bunch of outfitters regarding packs, and many of them have suggested that I stay away from packs with too many external pockets. My current pack definitely doesn't meet this criterion, but then, that's what I like about it. I also have an internal frame that is so streamlined that it takes me ten minutes to find what I want. It made packing a real miserable thing for me. When it comes to organization, it's either got to be easy to do or I just can't do it. On my recent hike I kept the weightier items in the base of the pack and the common-use lightweight things in the pockets. I absolutely loved having all the organization the external pockets allowed." Another hiker jokes that there may be definite psychological differences between hikers who prefer external vs. internal frame packs.

Rachel Dubois, Solophile, thru-hiked in '97 with her dog, Micah. "A woman should buy the smallest pack she can possibly stand. If your physical comfort level is carrying a pack with 35 pounds of gear, why in the world would you want to waste 20% or more of your precious pack weight on a 7 or 8 pound pack. Your pack is just a container! The bigger your pack, the more room you have for junk, i.e. extra weight."

"When I started the Trail, I began with a 5400 cu inches internal frame pack. It supposedly weighed 6 pounds 12 ounces. Before I left for Springer, I took the pack and cut off every extraneous buckle, tab, strap, pocket, and attachment. I even ditched the floating lid that was supposed to convert into a fanny pack because I didn't plan on slackpacking (hiking without a pack). When I was done with 'remodeling', the pack weighed 5 pounds 5 ounces and probably had about 4800 cu inches of capacity. Now I know you will cringe at the idea of mangling something that you just spent so much money for, but in my mind, I didn't want to carry anything for 2000+ miles that I wasn't going to use."

"By Harper's Ferry, the weather had warmed and I had switched to a summer sleeping bag and clothing. My pack had a lot of room in it that I just wasn't using. I decided to buy a 'summer' pack, a glorified weekend pack at about 3500 cu inches. The kicker was that it only weighed 3 pounds 5 ounces. It was wonderful. I carried a stove, filter, even a tent and my pack weight rarely exceeded 30 pounds. At times, when I was coming into town low on food, my pack weight was less than 20 pounds. Backpacking was a dream come true for me. My pack felt like a feather compared to some of the others hikers' packs. It really helped add to my enjoyment of the hike and allowed me to hike 1000+ miles in running shoes without any stress injuries."

Tents

The majority of women thru-hikers find that having a tent provides more camping options and privacy for changing and washing. With a tent they do not feel compelled to always hike to a shelter. Kathy Kelly Borowski, '88-'89, suggests, "My hiking partner left with the tent we were to share. After getting to a full shelter in the pouring rain, I had my tent shipped to me."

Beverly Hugo, Maine Rose, feels that having a tent adds to your freedom and flexibility. "I remember hiking with a couple north of Lehigh Gap with an impending storm brewing. They were faster than I was, so they continued on to the shelter. I stayed put a little off the Trail in a terrible thunder and lightning storm, dry in my tent and soothed by Elvis singing 'Kentucky Rain'." Rosie took a walkman from Harper's Ferry to Hanover and used it with earphones at night to listen to oldies rock & roll. Some women hike listening to music during the day while others find it distracts them from their surroundings.

Gail Johnson, Gutsy, '96, is a powerful confident hiker who quickly learned how to gauge her hiking abilities on the Trail. "I carried a tent when I began in March, but after a week or two of not using it (my plan was to stay in shelters) I sent it home and carried a nylon tarp instead. After a month of not using the tarp, I sent the tarp home. I did have my trusty rain poncho that was very useful as rain gear, ground cloth, pack cover, emergency tarp and windbreak on a cold, windy day. Before I began my hike I decided I would be the safest staying at shelters so I hiked until I reached the next shelter. Sometimes that meant hiking after dark. I think that the decreased weight from not carrying a tent helped me."

Sleeping Bags

Choose a sleeping bag by getting in it on the storeroom floor. Do you have wide hips, get claustrophobic in tight places, have a tendency for cold extremities or generally sleep cold? You may need to use two sleeping bags switching between a lightweight summer bag and a warmer down or poly bag for the cold ends of your hike. Follow Wingfoot's planning guide and handbook for suggested times and places to switch. If you are even minimally careful with your down bag putting the stuff sack or compression sack in a plastic garbage bag, you shouldn't have any problem keeping it dry. When washing your down bag, use a front loader washer not an agitator type, cold water, very mild detergent, and dry on a cool temp. See if the laundromat has a couple of tennis balls or a clean tennis shoe to throw in so the down will fluff up.

Too big a bag leaves too much space to warm. See if your outfitter has bags designed especially for women's body types. A sleeping bag is designed to keep you warm. Don't put a cold body in a cold bag. Eat or drink something warm before hitting your bag and make sure your body has generated a little heat especially in cold weather. Move around a bit or do some light exercise. Don't wear lots of clothes to bed and prevent the bag from doing its job. Petite women may find a good quality children's bag to be lighter weight and do the job effectively for their small body frames.

Jo-Ellen Kimmel, Mummyfoot, sometimes gets cold tootsies. She puts boiling water, tea bags, and sugar in a tightly sealed Nalgene bottle. She can warm her feet until she feels comfy and rehydrate throughout the night. Love your bag. There are days when you hit the sack at 6 p.m. or earlier and stay there for at least 12 hours. Hikers have been known to hole up in a shelter or their tent during a storm spending as much as a full day or more in their bags.

Sherri Swartz, Sunrise, solved the problem of zip-together sleeping bags that are versatile for different temperature ranges. She and her husband bought three summer weight semi-rectangular bags. "We zipped two together and kept them for the whole trip. The other one we used as a blanket and sent it home during the warmer months. It worked great. We were warm enough down to 20 degrees. The bags were lightweight and inexpensive and we got to sleep nice and comfy together."

Boots + Socks

According to an on-line internet "Consumer Reports," to the untrained eye, many hiking boots look the same. "A mediocre boot can look just as rugged as a good one-but even a good boot is a bad choice if it doesn't fit." Wear your hiking socks and shop in the afternoon or evening after your feet may have swelled. Allow about 1/2 inch between your longest toe and the boot tip. If you stand on tiptoes, the boot back should ride up with your heels, not slip down. Bring along an old pair of shoes to indicate wear pattern. Proper footwear is critical so shop with an experienced salesperson who deals with long distance hikers on a regular basis.

Many outfitters have a ramp you can walk up and down to get a slight inkling of what it might be like on those southern ups and downs. After you start your hike, you may find you need to add insoles or change the type of socks and liners. Many women thru-hikers use Thorlo socks alone; others prefer wool and liners or some other combination.

More important than either boot or sock choice, is what you do when you first feel a "hot spot" on the back of your heel. That is a call to STOP IMMEDIATELY. You must take heed. Let others forge ahead or ask a friend to hang back for a short break. Take off your pack. Get out your first aid Ziploc kept very handy for just such purposes rather than stuffed in the bottom of your pack. Take care of your feet, yourself, and the future of your hike! You and your feet come first. Have a small supply handy of Band-Aids, second skin, and moleskin so you can prevent serious problems later on.

Lisa Barter, Tinkerbell, wore running shoes for various stretches of her hike. "They were totally blown out by the time I finished, but I loved every step of the way." In other sections she wore boots for slogging through mud and for warmth. For steep, rocky and boulder filled areas, boots lend ankle stability. Needless to say, hiking with running shoes demands a light pack and an awareness of your foot, ankle, and leg strengths.

Hiking Sticks

Experienced thru-hikers have increasingly become aware that hiking with two sticks can ease the pressure on your knees for those strenuous southern descents. Some hikers hike with no sticks, some with one, and many with two. You can pick up a stick from the woods or purchase one making sure it has a rubber tip that will undoubtedly need replacing several times. High tech telescoping trekking poles have become more popular in recent years but there is some concern that when the rubber tip falls off, the metal points cause trail erosion.

Clothing

Stay away from cotton although some women like it for sleeping and town stops. Once wet from sweat or rain it never dries. Quick drying fabrics that wick away the moisture are preferred, although some women may not be able to wear materials made from petroleum by-products and chemicals. Hikers love fleece, but some hang on to the old wool sweater they've been hiking in for years. Section hiker, Gail M. Francis, gmf, was broke both times she hiked. "I didn't have any bells or whistles, but I managed to get

32

along fine with a wool sweater; make sure your hiking partner knows not to put wool sweaters in the dryer!" A warm fleece or wool hat for the duration is essential as are gloves. Raingear helps prevent hypothermia but coated nylon often works just as well as sweaty Gore-Tex.

Hikers love their bandannas often wearing one on their heads to cover their hair and to catch the sweat. Attaching one to a pack strap for wiping a runny nose is helpful. Women will need to learn to blow their noses by holding the sides of their nostrils. It's not a ladylike sight, but it saves on toilet paper that has more essential uses.

Bras and undies are a hot topic for women hikers. Although some women can go braless while hiking, larger breasted women are continually in search for the sportsbra that doesn't make them look like they have one spreading horizontal breast across their chest. Look for one with an underwire support although one hiker reports that the wire gouged into her body. Synthetic shorts with integral panties are cool, don't bind, and dry easily. Choose a wicking fabric and peruse catalogs from various companies.

Lisa Barter, Tinkerbell, explains her system for trail undies. "After hiking from Springer to North Carolina carrying four or five pairs of undies, I found I liked the following system: carry one pair of simple black nylon undies with cotton crotch from Victoria's Secret for wear in towns or under pants. Carry two pairs of ultra-lightweight running shorts with integral liners, one by Reebok, and the other by Moving Comfort, which I got through REI. I'd start with two clean pairs; wear one pair the first day, then wash the crotch with a little Dr. Bonner's peppermint oil soap and hang to dry. In the morning, I'd put on the other pair and leave the washed one on my pack to dry. Then every day I'd have a mostly clean pair to wear, but no undies to worry about. On really cold days I'd wear a pair of shorts with black wind pants over them. The lightweight materials worked really well, especially for ventilation. I found that wearing tight undies under another layer proved irritating to my crotch because of too little air circulation. I carried one cotton/lycra bra and one t-back bra, and switched them off. That never seemed to be a problem."

Women & Thru-Hiking on the Appalachian Trail

A recent thru-hiker took another approach. "I carried six pairs of underwear, which some other hikers teased me about, but I always had a clean, dry pair every day. They weighed almost nothing and, to me, the extra few ounces were worth it. I hate wearing the same sweaty clothes every day. I can deal with dirty/sweaty shorts, shirts, and hair, but clean underwear is a health necessity as well as a luxury." Women whose thighs rub together when walking are advised to wear snug fitting boxer undies that don't inch their way up.

Tracey Parizek, Oasis, designed and wore "hiking" dresses of stretch supplex material during her '98 thru-hike. She shortened patterns for loose fitting high waisted dresses with either gathered or pleated skirts. The hemlines were four inches above the knee, modest, and extremely comfortable. Under the skirts, Tracey also made her own design for bike shorts complete with a pocket for money and chapstick. "Bike shorts are great, but I don't like the bike short/t-shirt look." Tracey found the material cool but it didn't flow and stuck to her at times.

Her next forays into the world of women's hiking clothing design will include shorts of slippery lycra and dresses of rayon. "Rayon would actually be cheaper than technical fabric and it dries fairly fast. Just make sure you wash it several times before sewing so it's completely pre-shrunk. Then you'll be able to wash it in laundromats in trail towns with no problems." Tracey's wardrobe also included a rayon sarong from Indonesia that she used as a bag liner/sheet/wrap around skirt in town. She observed that several girls switched to skirts or dresses in the summer months.

Many hikers at the '98 Trailfest in Hot Springs admired another woman's hiking dress attire. Theresa Beachy, a young Mennonite woman and '98 thru-hiker, also wore a hiking dress of her own design. Perhaps Tracey and Theresa will start a new trend in women's AT wear.

A woman has hundreds of combinations from which to choose those few items that will be her wardrobe for six months, more or less. If something doesn't work, send it home and get something else along the way. Nothing is cast in stone. What is right for you and your particular needs, keeping packweight as a major consideration, may not be what is best for another woman.

34

Women & Thru-Hiking on the Appalachian Trail

Women today can choose from a myriad of options in outdoor apparel often hiking in shorts and halter-tops made of lightweight, quick drying, synthetic wicking fabrics. In the 1800's this would hardly have been considered "proper attire" for ladies. According to Tina Roberts, who has researched early Maine women active in conservation efforts, women needed to be liberated from their hemlines (Lagasse, M. A. (1997, August 8.) Women in the wilderness. Bangor Daily News, pp. C5-C6).

Tina relates a story about a party of people including women hiking Katahdin in 1855. "The men all sported sturdy and comfortable combinations of shirts and frocks. On the other hand, one woman wore a chocolate brown suit corded with scarlet, a white felt hat, and was described by her male guide as looking like 'Little Bo Peep.' Despite her clumsy attire, it was the woman who first reached the top and prodded the gentlemen to continue."

Katahdin is considered to be the single most difficult climb on the Appalachian Trail. On August 11, 1849, two women, Elizabeth Oakes Smith, 42, of Portland, Maine and a Mrs. N.C. Mosman (or Bosman) of Bangor, Maine climbed the state's highest mountain, the northern terminus of the AT. They forged streams and clambered over boulders in floor length skirts to become the first women to summit Katahdin, 82 years before Baxter State Park was established.

In the neighboring state of New Hampshire more than 30 years later, adventurous women reveled in the challenging terrain of the White Mountains. Peter Rowan and June Hammond Rowan, have collected letters and diaries of four extraordinary women. Described as "astonishingly strong climbers," they wore long full skirts or dresses while hiking and wrote of their exploits in the Appalachian Mountain Club Journal, Appalachia. (Rowan, P., & Rowan, J.H. (1995) Mountain Summers: Tales of hiking and exploration in the White Mountains from 1878 to 1886 as seen through the eyes of women. Gorham, NH: Gulfside Press).

One friend writes to another, "Do you mind telling me how Miss Cook and you manage to climb trees so readily without dropping your dress skirts?" The response, "Consider first that the middle sized spruces were conveniently branched down to the ground. The getting up is very easy as

35

the skirts came naturally after. A graceful descent is more difficult, as the same skirts are apt to remain above, but my uncle and Mr. Peek considerately left, so that grace did not have to be considered."

Women also just couldn't pick up the phone and call a 1-800 number for easy ordering and delivering. "Miss Whitman's dress…was a dark blue flannel down to her boot tops and a rather long half fitting sack belted in, relieved with a little white trimming. I should think that for underbrush Miss Whitman must use something stronger than flannel. My aunt and I found some nice fine woolen jean in Gorham for which she looked in vain in New York."

Such formality and decorum! It didn't keep them out of the woods or prevent them from above treeline excursions. They got dirty, sweaty, and grubby and had a deep spiritual appreciation for all that surrounded them.

Reflections of a 2x thru-hiker

Two-time thru-hiker Ginny Owen, Spirit Walker, reflects on going "lite" after watching Lynn Wheldon's video on ultra-light backpacking.

One of the points that was made in the video that really rang a bell with me was his point that packweight and fear are directly related. The more fear you are carrying, the more weight you will carry. If you are afraid of being cold, you will bring an extra sweater. If you are afraid of being hungry, you will bring extra food. If you are afraid of injury, you will bring a big first aid kit. If you are afraid of boredom, you will bring cards or a book. If you fear disaster, you will bring a cell phone.

With experience, as you see that most of the things that you feared either don't happen or are not that difficult to live with, you begin to lighten both your fear and your pack load. Look at a thru-hiker's first aid kit at the end of the Trail-not much there. The only thing that got used was the moleskin and ibuprofen, so everything else gets tossed. They stop being afraid. Look at how many get rid of water filters, deciding they can endure the taste of iodine, and that giardia, while extremely nasty, probably won't kill you. A cold wet night becomes an adventure, rather than the end of the world, so it doesn't matter if the tent leaks a bit. You get used to going to bed at dusk, so cold nights aren't much to worry about. You just jump in the sleeping bag as soon as you hit camp. I want to be out backpacking in my 60's and 70's. That means I have to lighten up. At the moment 25-30 pounds isn't unbearable, but 20 would be better.

I was thinking about my early days as a backpacker. I had no money, no experience, and no gear. I went out and had a good time anyway. Now that I have a little money, a lot more experience, and too much gear, I'm trying to get back to the simplicity with which I started. It isn't easy. When I watched Wheldon's video, and when I read some of the ideas on the on-line mailing lists, I kept thinking, "I can't do that," sometimes because it isn't "safe" or sometimes because it is less "comfortable." This comes down to letting my fears, including fears of being uncomfortable (like carrying a tent instead of a tarp because I don't like getting bitten by mosquitoes) determine my hike. That isn't acceptable. I need to listen every time I think "I can't" and ask again, "Well, why not?" If it is because of fear, well, I have never believed in letting fear rule my life.

Ginny feels that the only truly essential gear is attitude and that isn't gender specific.

Chapter two

DURING

I am Woman

Melissa Sumpter, Selky, writes from the Trail. "We're all part of one big family out here. We all help where we can to make this life more bearable. And what a life it is! Especially for women. We are an important link in the cycle of life. Too often we are dehumanized and made to be sex objects for commercials and TV. We are made into objects of desire, unworthy of respect. Well, that's not how the real world works. We are strong, capable humans demanding respect. I have found that out here people recognize the difficulty of the tasks we are able to perform. They dig deeper than looks. This helps you to forget what you look like and find out who you are. You find strength and power in being female. You are a creator with the ability to give life. That makes you amazing. Walking alone over Mother Earth has helped me to realize that it's given me a sense of strength I never knew, an unparalleled empowered feeling of capability. I can climb that hill. I can walk those miles. I WILL make it to Maine!"

Jane Marriott, Pokey, echoes Selky's sentiments. "You are a woman. You are privileged to belong to the sisterhood of all women. We are beings who value process, individuality, unity, beauty, and creativity. We are empathic, nurturing, understanding, and forgiving. As women we have much in common, but we women on the Trail have even more in common-a special bond. You will find female companionship along the Trail. Women are usually quick to share and develop friendship easily. You already have pals on the trip you haven't even made yet. Use your female connections-"this book for instance"-to gather the information and courage to move forward. Implore the women in your life to understand and support you. Know that you have a base on the Trail and a base at your home. Smile and go."

Is it "absolutely" safe for a woman to hike the AT?

All women, let alone women hikers, know that it is not absolutely safe for any woman anywhere. Contributors were eager to provide their opinions and suggestions for maximizing a woman's personal safety under Trail conditions. In the history of the Trail there have been nine murders of both women and men, hiking solo, with a partner, with and without a dog. Rape, although uncommon, does occur. Violent crimes such as these have been perpetrated, predominantly, from outside the thru-hiking community. Many women thru-hikers agree that one of the safest Trail situations is being a woman alone in a shelter with a bunch of sweaty, reaking, crotch scratching, snoring, belching, farting male testosterone driven thru-hikers. We bless their presence on the Trail and the energy, love, and support they bring to our experience.

Kelly Winters, Amazin' Grace, '96 writes, "It is not absolutely safe for a woman, or a man for that matter, to do anything, in the woods or in the city. There is no safety in this world. You could sit home all your life thinking you're 'safe', but you could have cancer and be dying from the inside out, right there in your comfortable chair, without even knowing it. I think both men and women should take every reasonable precaution to ensure their safety, but should not let fear keep them from living fully,

40

reaching out, and moving along. That includes hiking the Trail."

"Hiking a great distance, I was stronger, both physically and mentally. My senses were sharper. You develop a good danger detector. You see things very clearly, and this helps you protect yourself before anything ever happens. In the city, most people seem like they're sleepwalking, easy victims. In the woods, you're awake and clear. You're strong. Most rapists and those who would hassle you are looking for someone weak. If you hike far enough, you won't be. Most criminals are lazy, not likely to hike 20 miles through mountains to find a victim. Most crimes occur near roads. Be wary of roads and it will do a lot to keep you safe."

Jean Arthur expresses her perspective. "It is never absolutely safe to do anything, and wouldn't life be a humdrum affair if it were? We would be just existing if we had no adventures and never experienced any thrills. One of our modern fallacies is trying to make life perfectly safe." Jean hiked the Trail over a nine-year period, the last two after retirement, mostly with her husband whom she met on the AT through her hiking group.

"The answer is...absolutely not," emphasizes Sue Freeman, Blueberry. "It is also not absolutely safe for a woman to walk from her house to her car. It is not absolutely safe for her to drive from her car to the local shopping mall nor is it absolutely safe for her to walk from her car to the mall. And yet, we do these things regularly. A thru-hike is no safer and no less safe than any other activity we choose to pursue in life. In each case there are things we can do personally to increase our measure of safety."

Courtney Mann, Mojo, expresses strong sentiments regarding advising women about trail dangers. "If a woman has to be told how she may avoid being in dangerous or risky situations on the Trail, she does not belong out there. Let's not make it easy for people who do not have the confidence, self-reliance, and tenacity to undertake something as gargantuan as an AT thru-hike." Courtney also feels that if a woman needs to read a book about thru-hiking to ascertain whether she can do it as a woman, she probably does not belong on the Trail.

Jeanne Spellman found sharing space to be very safe as long as she trusted her instincts about situations to avoid. "I never had a problem at a town hostel. I should note that I am generally friendly toward male hikers and enjoyed their company. I met a lot of male thru-hikers on the Trail, and while I occasionally met some real jerks, I never felt unsafe in their company. I found that most male thru-hikers were very protective toward women traveling alone. My fears came from dealing with local hunters or once, a weekend hiker."

Jeanne suggests hikers sign the registers and try to be entertaining so that people follow you and care about you. "Signing the registers is equally important if your plans change. I left the Trail with an injury and didn't write that in a register or arrange for anyone else to write it for me. Many people I didn't know worried about my 'disappearance'."

Dot MacDonald, D-Trail, writes, "I refuse to be held hostage to fear or evil. I will hike my own hike, however it occurs, be it alone or with others. I can't let things that may happen interfere with the unfolding of the adventure. If we are someone who has experienced violence and cannot ignore the fear, then perhaps a dog as a companion, lessons in self-defense, or a handy container of mace might help. I would encourage as little alteration in your plans as possible. God knows, as women the constraints are tight enough between family and society's expectations than to carry them in our backpacks as well. Think free and rely on our biological gift of intuition to steer clear of danger."

Carolyn Cunningham, Tawanda, reflects on her thru-hike at age 19. "Absolutely safe on the AT? This question assumes that the AT is a separate world than the so-called 'real world,' the world of houses and cars. The AT is not a mystical place that exists outside of society. Instead, the people that one comes in contact with represent all aspects of society including those who are racist, misogynist, sexist, and homophobic. Women should realize that while the Trail can be an empowering experience, it can also be a frustrating one. Common sense and street smarts should always be exercised while hiking the Trail. Hikers and members of the Trail community care very much about other hikers and look out for each other. They look at register entries, send messages up and down the Trail, and become a part of one's family. This sense of community and protection is hard to find outside of the Trail."

Women &Thru-Hiking on the Appalachian Trail

"Too often society tells women that we cannot do things by ourselves, such as wear certain types of clothing or go out alone at night. If we do these things, then we can expect to be attacked and possibly blamed for it. This is often the truth in court cases. The Trail can be an empowering experience for women because they find safety in the wilderness. I never had any reason to be afraid on the AT. But, as we can see from the violent incidents that have occurred on or near the AT, it is a reality that violence towards women does exist. Rather than telling women that it is not safe, or that we should arm ourselves against potential wierdoes, or we should curb our actions 'in case something may happen,' we should seek to educate each other about how to use common sense and avoid potentially dangerous situations. In this way, we can affect positive change for women and men on the Trail."

"I had left the Trail to go to my sister's graduation and I was just getting back on," writes Dania Egedi, Lightweight. PBK (Peanut Butter Kid) and Rasta-Bear passed me as I was getting suited back up. The Trail there left town, went up and over a ridge, and then crossed a gravel road before hitting the woods for good. As I came off the ridge to cross the road Rasta-Bear was waiting for me. It turned out that as he and PBK came to the crossing, there was a guy in a pick-up waiting there, drinking and throwing beer cans out the window. They didn't feel comfortable knowing that I was about 20 minutes behind them, and decided to 'take a break' there. After about 10 minutes, the guy left, and they waited until I came through before heading on. Was the guy trouble? I have no idea, but it was nice being part of a community that cared about each other."

Dania adds, "My mother was extremely nervous about me hiking the Trail. I kept telling her to stop worrying. After my hike, I moved to Philadelphia. I called her and told her to start worrying! I was in much greater danger there than I ever was on the Trail."

A Missouri hiker writes, "No it's not absolutely safe. Nothing is absolutely safe. However, I hiked 1700 miles of the AT solo, and the fears that people had for me-rape, abduction, theft, or whatever-were entirely unfounded. I didn't feel threatened by the people I met while hiking, hitching, or going about towns, and I didn't carry any sort of protective

43

devices (phone, mace, gun, etc.) My belief was that if I went onto the Trail afraid of who I might meet, I wasn't going to be able to trust people or form good friendships. My experience on the Trail was that people were helpful and generous even when they were not people I particularly liked."

"What I really feared was physical safety. I really worried about severe injuries especially on high ridges and when rock hopping in the rain. What I found was that I could control that fear by adjusting my hiking. If it was raining and I was afraid of falling, I'd stop early for the day. If I got scared I'd stop and take a break. My advice would be that you'll get scared by the terrain at some point, and when it happens you have to keep going."

Anne Mausolff, The Green Mountaineer, wisely suggests that, "One must acknowledge possibilities and gauge the probabilities and sometimes take a calculated risk. Take full responsibility for one's words, actions, and non-actions. Much depends on the 'aura' a woman projects around herself: diffident, shy, victim-minded, self-assured, resolute… ready to defend herself if need be."

Carrying "Protection"

The majority of successful women thru-hikers responding to the survey and questionnaire were not part of the on-line women's listserve and were unaware of debates about protection on the Trail. We asked if women need a gun, pepper spray, MACE, cell-phone, or a dog to be safe. Some wrote that they felt the question was absurd. The survey called for a check mark, but several women couldn't resist adding their own personal responses such as: "Oh, please!," "Give me a break!," "If a woman feels she needs this kind of protection, she should stay home," or "It's (cell phone) absolutely ridiculous and an annoyance for other hikers."

Almost no women took a dog primarily for protection and the use of cell phones was negligible. The acceptable use for cell phones is to use it, as recommended on the Trailplace website, in the same places where you would have a bowel movement. That doesn't mean at gorgeous lookouts, "Hey, honey, guess where I am now" or in a shelter area where folks are chatting and preparing a meal. Cell phones are totally inappropriate for a wilderness setting, and you can't get a connection half the time anyway. Besides, it's packweight you don't need.

That gun you have, the one buried in your pack, is against the law in many areas and could easily be used against you. "Carrying a gun is carrying fear. Guns are heavy, dangerous, and illegal on the Trail." A few years ago section hiker, Susanne Wright Ashland, did her first three-day trip alone in the Maine woods. "My son insisted I carry a small gun. That gun and I did not get along! If during the day I had run into anyone wishing to harm me, I never would have gotten the gun out in time to defend myself. I sure did not relish the idea of walking with it in my hand or pocket so it would be handy...just in case. At night I slept with it in my sleeping bag and was afraid that I would hit the safety and then discharge the gun therefore shooting myself as I sleep."

Only 11% of 2000 milers surveyed took pepper spray. There is a legitimate fear of dogs both on and off the Trail. One hiker always picked up a few stones on her way into town. Pepper spray seems the least obtrusive of any self-protective device and a woman needs to learn which direction to point it. If she plans on ever using it, she needs to keep it someplace that is easily accessible like on a strap or in small fanny pack worn on the front of her body.

Dogs twice attacked a thru-hiker carrying pepper spray but she just "yelled like a total maniac and flailed my hiking sticks." One woman added that she sent it home after 30 miles at Neel's Gap, another said that she never took it out of her pack, and a third lost hers in Pennsylvania...or was it New Jersey? No woman ever reported using pepper spray in self-defense on man or beast. "There is nothing you could have that someone bigger and stronger wouldn't be able to take and turn back on you." A hiker started taking karate after finishing her thru-hike so she would feel safer hiking alone. "Unfortunately, my knees did so much better when I stopped karate, that I never got to the point that I could be shown how to use the techniques with a pack on."

What common sense precautions
should a woman exercise on a thru-hike?

Hiker after hiker echoed the same sentiments as Kyra Sotter, Purple Haze, '97 thru-hiker. "Follow your intuition! You'd be surprised at how your sixth sense comes alive when the other senses are no longer overloaded by all the intense stimuli out there. People really do put off vibes. Go with your gut."

Women have been socialized to be "nice," "polite," "to follow the rules." When thru-hiking the AT, a woman's first concern should be for her own personal safety. Jeanne Spellman feels the most important precaution is to trust yourself and the little voice that says, "This isn't safe." "Be willing to be rude, to pack up and leave if you have a bad feeling about a shelter or the people in it. One night I had finished cooking my supper and a man arrived who gave me a creepy feeling. I was casual and polite, hastily ate my supper, packed up my things and said, 'I'm going to make a few more miles tonight.' I hiked for about 25 minutes and pitched my tent out of sight from the Trail." Be prepared, even when dead tired or wet and cold, to hike on another mile or two. You can always eat a cold supper and dry breakfast if your safety is a consideration.

A tent site a couple of hundred feet off the Trail out of sight, especially one without a fire ring and signs of obvious use, is a safe place for a woman to pitch her tent if she decides not to go to a designated shelter area. It also helps if the color of the tent can blend in with natural surroundings. There are locations on the Trail where it is officially forbidden to camp. Although most thru-hikers try to get to either official shelter areas or campsites, it may be impossible to do so. No woman should ever compromise her personal safety in such a situation. When tired and unable to continue, she should stealth camp several hundred feet off the Trail making as little disturbance to the area as possible. Just because someone else is a faster hiker and can make it to a designated shelter, is not a good enough reason for pushing beyond safety considerations for yourself.

Emily Reith, Bugbite, was a little paranoid the first time she found herself alone at night. "After I set up my camp well off the Trail, I went back to the Trail and walked up and down a bit to be sure my campsite could not be seen. After doing that, I felt very relaxed in my tent and had one of the best night's sleep without the noises of the other hikers."

Beverly Hugo, Maine Rose, stopped cooking in Tennessee. "Not cooking was initially an effort to save packweight and became a joke about my non-domestic nature. The Trail gets a whole lot simpler when you don't even have a pot to wash, although you do have to kick the coffee habit. The real safety benefit for me, personally, was being able to dry camp. As a slow solo hiker, I felt it imperative to stop before dark and set up camp. I found the Trail challenging enough, thank you, without adding night hiking to my new repertoire of skills. I wasn't compelled to get to a shelter for water or to a water source. This kept the stress of pushing on in check and proved an effective way of taking care of myself. Water needs for a cold camp are greatly below those for cooking and washing up."

A young solo woman hiker almost got herself in trouble by writing how lonely she was in a Trail register. She signed her Trailname clearly identifying herself as a woman. Some solo women take non-gender related Trailnames, a unisex handle. A very strange shelter caretaker ended up harassing her causing her much discomfort and stress, if no real harm, and teaching her a lesson in protecting herself from seeming vulnerable. Hikers, both male and female, need to protect solo women by not mentioning their plans. A chance remark either on the Trail or in a town can put a woman in danger. When hiking solo, don't advertise it to strangers on the Trail. Tell them your husband, partner, or friends are right behind you. Be vague. If a stranger comes along, ask if he's seen… naming names of hikers...and that you're waiting for them. Don't chitchat and make small talk.

Be especially careful at road crossings. Check things out before you cross making sure there are no cars in the vicinity. If in doubt, wait back in the trees until another hiker shows up and evaluate the situation together.

Some women feel more secure attaching a whistle to one of their front pack straps to be used ONLY in an emergency. Like inconsiderate use of cell phones, a whistle tooting away in the woods as a signal to a friend is totally inappropriate for a wilderness setting.

Don't camp or stay in shelters near roads unless you are with a group of thru-hikers. There is definitely safety in numbers in these situations but shelters close to the road are magnets for local parties that often include alcohol. If you are the first person in the shelter area, don't unpack all your things until you are sure you are going to stay the night. That way, if you feel uncomfortable with someone who shows up, you can throw on your pack and head out.

Barbara DiGiovanni, D-Boss, has some general safety tips. "When tenting, check the surrounding area for loose limbs if there is a big storm coming. I knew of someone who set up his tent, went to sleep, and in the middle of the night left the tent to answer nature's call. While he was out all of two minutes, a tree fell on his tent. A guardian angel was watching out for him. Don't set up your tent in a dell or depression. If it rains you will be soaked and even in summer if you have a cool night you could get hypothermia. A first priority of any camping is to stay dry. Make sure you have dry clothes in your pack wrapped in Ziplocs. Don't cook in your tent; they catch fire easily and the food smells attract critters."

Cleo Wolf, Footloose, '91, was at a shelter in Tennessee where the locals were reported to hate hikers. "Late at night I heard footsteps, step-step, step-step. It was pitch black out. Who could be walking around but someone who knows this mountain like the back of his hand? The hostile coughed a little and walked closer. Another hiker shone a flashlight out and caught him in the light; a deer, startled and indignant, glared back."

Hitchhiking

The majority of women thru-hiking the Trail have never hitchhiked. Despite all we know about the dangers of such a practice, women need to come to terms with the fact that hitchhiking will, at some point during a thru-hike, be a necessity. Why? Unlike Trail towns such as Hot Springs, North Carolina and Damascus, Virginia where the Trail passes right through town and the blazes are painted on telephone poles, many of the locations for resupply are too far away from the Trail to walk. If there is one thing a thru-hiker does not want to do is add too many additional miles to weary feet. So hitchhiking is inevitable.

If a woman decides to solo, she already has a mindset that she will handle whatever the Trail offers up for experience. That includes hitchhiking. Although one could wait for another hiker to guarantee further safety, a solo woman will need to decide if she is really going to go the distance as planned or end up being dependent on another hiker for her sense of security. Going solo is a package deal. It involves planning alone, often tenting alone, hiking without someone waiting for you at the shelter, negotiating difficult terrain by yourself, and hitchhiking alone, if necessary.

As Kelly Winters, Amazin' Grace, suggests, "Your attitude can help you. If you are strong, resilient, and are not a pushover, potential jerks will sense this and look for an easier mark. Obviously, if you're a woman considering hiking alone, the odds are that you are like this. Go with it. Don't take a ride if the person gives you bad vibes. You get vibes for a reason. Pay attention to them and you'll be safe. Ignore them, and you will be placing yourself in danger. Just say, 'Oh, I've changed my mind,' or something like that. Don't let anyone convince you to get into a car if you don't feel right about it. If the person really is a dangerous jerk, he may swear at you or try to convince you to get in the car: further proof it's a good idea not to. But so what? Curses are gone in a cloud of dust and you still have your life."

The first time Kay Cutshall, The Old Gray Goose, ever hitchhiked was in Georgia and she was alone. "I just figured if I really didn't feel at ease with the person who stopped, I'd think of something to say for not going with them. Actually I haven't ended up hitching on my own very often. It just happened that I would be with someone else when I got to the road to hitch or I would leave the shelter with someone with plans to hitch to town together."

"Avoid extremes," warns section hiker, Shari Galvez, Second Chance. "You may be the most intuitive and perceptive woman in the world. However, extremes will not help that process. Don't get TOO hot. Don't get TOO cold. Don't get TOO fatigued. Don't get TOO hungry. Don't get TOO thirsty. Your decision-making can, and probably will, be hampered by any of these extremes. One beautiful morning on hitching a ride to town with a bad knee, bronchitis, and fatigue, I realized afterwards that if Charles Manson had offered me a ride, I would have taken it. Don't let any kind of 'Charlie' pick you up because you haven't taken care of what you could take care of before reaching your desperation point."

Section hiker Donna Savluk, Ward's Girl, suggests always staying near the AT crossing and having your pack visible. "Someone will stop in a short amount of time since the people in the AT towns are somewhat used to giving rides to hikers. Trust your gut and don't get into a car if you feel apprehensive about any of the vehicle's occupants. I have occasion to cross the AT in my vehicle several times a week. I will always pick up the hiker with a backpack standing at the crossing but never the hitchhiker that is a mile from the crossing with no backpack."

Cleo Wolf, Footloose, warns, "Do not flirt-the first rule of hitchhiking. Bring your backpack; look like a hiker. After several weeks of hiking, we do look like hikers and without that clear label on our back there is some difficulty for others to decide what seems different about you. Is it the walk? The look on the face? Are you a bum or what? Trust your instincts. Always, always, always listen to that little voice in your head and stay off drugs and booze when hitching." Taking note of the license number of the car or truck is also recommended.

Linda Ivey, Mountain Mama, discusses trust. "Having been a social worker for 20 years has caused me to develop a suspicious nature. Sweet little old ladies, parents, and child molesters have lied to me. So I would be pretty stupid to get in a car with strangers, right? Thank heaven I've had a series of crazy incidents while section hiking the AT to cause me to depend on really strange people. I have been stranded next to interstates after dark, left to find a way home at the wrong place in the freezing cold, and scared to death on a side road near Mahoosuc Notch. Each time several strangers have come to the rescue. I have gotten into pickups with good old boys and strange talking northerners. Lots of people have gone out of their way to help a dirty hiker, and they have had more reason to be worried than I have. I would never take safety for granted, and prefer riding with couples in a pick-up truck, but so far have had good experiences with people. Hitchhiking is my last choice and I prefer making arrangements with listed shuttle providers servicing section hikers, but hope I can continue expecting good out of people when emergencies arise."

Rachel Dubois, Solophile, answered a woman on the list who asked if it was possible to do all the AT without hitchhiking. "Yes, it's possible, but you'll have to plan your hike much more carefully and meticulously. Many of the Trail towns are only a few miles away and those distances can definitely be covered on foot. Road miles are very tiring ones. I'd rather walk two miles in the woods than a mile on the road. The pounding your feet take on road surfaces when you walk them in boots and with a pack is phenomenal."

"Another important issue is, while you're walking on a road, you are also exposed to passersby. I don't think roadwalks are a great idea, especially if you do them alone. Whenever I knew I had a roadwalk coming up, I would always try and arrange to do it together with another hiker. Once I left the comfort and perceived safety of the woods, I was always much more apprehensive and concerned for my safety. At least with a hitchhike, you get to pick with whom to go. Although it might be difficult to tactfully turn down a ride when you don't feel comfortable with the person who offered it, it can be done if you're creative. When you're doing a roadwalk, you're exposed to everyone who drives by."

Thru-hiking gave Christine Shaw, Firefly, her first shot at hitching. "Pretty scary, but at the time it saved my life. I was in a horrible winter storm, and the temperature was below zero. Eventually, I got comfortable catching a ride with strangers and hitched alone on several occasions though I avoided it when I could. Most of the women I met did have to hitch alone at one point or another. Most of the people who pick up hikers on the road were friends of the AT. Usually they pick up hikers every season, and sometimes you get lucky and they'd offer you a home-cooked dinner. It would always happen when you needed it the most."

Some women thru-hikers make hitching an event in and of itself. Kelly Winters, Amazin' Grace, knows the techniques for finding a ride and how to enjoy it. "I was paranoid about hitching alone. Generally, there were enough other hikers around that I could arrange to hitch into town with others, often big guys. It was a benefit to both of us. Guys sometimes don't get rides when they're alone, but if they're with a woman, it makes them look less threatening to drivers. It also makes the woman safer from potential bad folks. Nothing is guaranteed, though. If a driver has a gun, you could both be in big trouble."

Kelly, like most thru-hikers, preferred to hitch in pickup trucks, riding in the back rather than up front with the driver. Remember to keep a hold of your gear as you are getting in rather than tossing your pack in ahead of you. You can keep an eye on your pack (it isn't locked up in someone's trunk), and not be confined in a small space with the driver. Kelly did note that she was fine on those occasions when she was up front. "I often chose the person I wanted to give me a ride by going up to people at tourist places where the Trail crosses a road (like Newfound Gap in the Smokies), and chat with them. That way, you check them out, they know you're not a nut, and when you ask for a ride, both of you know what you're dealing with."

"In New England, I would ask people in the grocery store if they would mind giving me a ride up the road after I had watched them for a while and spoken with them. Generally people are curious about your big pack and will start conversations with you, and you can explain what you're doing and mention you need a ride. Or, they're familiar with the Trail and know that hikers often hitch."

"I never had a bad experience hitching and in fact, met some wonderful people; a New York city psychiatrist, another woman who did therapy with dogs and horses, a man whose son died on Everest, a Mainer who wanted to move to Alaska and then have Alaska secede from the US, an old Southern gentleman with a dog who could sing, some punk-rock teenagers who had a lot to say about their town, a woman with 13 cats (we stopped at her house to visit them), and a whole lot of others. It was really an interesting part of the trip."

Linda Patton, Earthworm, has also made connections with drivers. "My hitchhiking experience comes from section hiking. I would expect it to be even more of a necessity on a thru-hike. I've done it four times when I was hiking alone and had to get back to my car when my hike was interrupted by illness or injury. I had thought of what I was going to say if

I wanted to turn down an offer…if the potential angel looked more like the devil! Three times a couple stopped for me; one even had kids in the car. The fourth time it was two women. I didn't see any danger signs. I just sent some Florida fruit to my most recent angels as a thank you because they drove me a long distance. I'll have to admit that the first time was a bit nerve-wracking, but after that, I sort of took it in stride."

Sue Kenn, White Glove, warns not to leave your pack in a vehicle while you go into a store or post office unless the driver is going in with you or unless you really feel confident that the driver is trustworthy. Even an experienced hiker like Sue can make a bad judgment. "We were trying to hitch a ride into town when a man in a jeep Cherokee stopped. We loaded our packs and poles into the back which wasn't easy due to all the other stuff back there. (mistake number one) Before the driver even started to pull out into the road, he held up a wine bottle and asked if we wanted a drink. We said no thanks and just sat there. (mistake number two)"

"Why didn't we get out? He proceeded down the road swerving and almost going off the road several times. After a few miles of this frightening ride, we all pointed up the road to a house on the right and hollered, 'that's where we want to go!' He eventually landed partly on the lawn and we quickly got out. I walked to the rear of the vehicle and threw packs and poles onto the lawn. It took me 24 hours to get over this ride. I will never make this mistake again. I was thinking more about getting into town and not whether this was a good ride or not."

Are lesbians in any more danger on the AT because of their sexual orientation?

The Trail is still a microcosm of society despite whatever idealism we attribute to it. Hate crimes on or near the Trail have resulted in the murders of three lesbian short-term hikers in two different incidents. Two women, experienced hikers accompanied by their dog, were brutally murdered on a side trail near the AT in '96. In '88 another woman was gunned down while her partner, Claudia Brenner, miraculously survived. Her book, Eight Bullets, describes their horrifying ordeal.

Women & Thru-Hiking on the Appalachian Trail

In the process of writing this book, the women on the WATL, Women's Appalachian Trail List, as well as those who answered the questionnaire, have come forward in a sincere effort to address a situation that affects all women. We want all women to be safe on the AT whatever their sexual orientation, but unfortunately, specific added precautions may need to be taken. Each woman will have to judge for herself if verbally expressing her orientation, showing a tattoo, or displaying a badge on her pack is worth the risk. Straight women cannot divorce themselves from their responsibility for concern for their fellow hikers' safety. Many women hike together on the Trail as friends as well as partners in a relationship. The perception of a hate monger, whether on the Trail or in a town, does not differentiate.

What has been made clear in our discussions is that simply stated, sexual orientation is not about sex. That is the same whether lesbian or straight. Sex is a private affair. A list member writes, "The question is about safety...not about sex! Safety is about violence, not about decorum, and not about public displays of affection." Another hiker cautions against broadcasting any "liberal" positions in some of the smaller conservative towns. "If you decide to out of conviction or integrity, just don't be naïve. There's risk of the wrong person hearing."

Straight women freely share details of home and family openly discussing their feelings for their missed loved ones. A '91 hiker definitely felt less supported and shut out after she came "out" and that means a lot on the Trail where hikers look out for each other. "The danger is, if you are 'out', you may not have that support from other hikers. They may not wait for you at road crossings to hitch together or keep the tone of conversations and jokes safe for you as well as them. Other hikers may not invite you to go with them to eat or share a room or even share information about places and people. The same dangers lurk everywhere as well as callousness, hostility, and disregard of your feelings. There is always the risk of being targeted by some nutso and shunned by fellow hikers. Thru-hikers aren't just hungry for food but also hungry for talk and whom we love is a big issue. It comes into discussions about cars, kitchens, pets, and gardening."

A hiker suggests, "Deciding what to tell to whom must be tempered by the environment and the available recourse if you get an unexpected reaction. In other words, if you are on a city bus, you can just get off at the next stop, but if you are in a shelter five miles from the nearest road, you have limited alternatives." This is the sad reality.

Another list member urges straight women hikers to accept and not judge their gay counterparts in this wilderness adventure. We can support each other and set an example for others. "Lesbians face a double threat of attack and harassment in the outdoors because they are women and because they are lesbians."

"I never got directly hassled about it. I almost never felt comfortable being out or even entering into conversations about sexuality with anyone other than other lesbians. For a little while I hiked with one other lesbian and a macho-type guy and after hearing him rant homophobically for a few days, we finally had a talk with him about it (heart stopping) and he actually was pretty cool and admitted he was mostly scared about it because he had a gay brother."

A '96 thru-hiker states, "It is a sad fact that lesbians are in danger because of their sexual orientation both on and off the Trail. Being 'out' on the Trail may not be a good idea, simply because the hiking community is very gossipy. Gossip weighs nothing, so it's the easiest thing to carry up the Trail. Once your story is past your lips, you can't control it. You never know who will hear that you are a lesbian and how strangely they may react when they run into you. Most hikers are fine, but since they represent a cross-section of society, there are some homophobes and jerks among them. You may end up alone in a shelter with one of these people or run into them when you're alone on the Trail. In addition, the Trail passes through rural areas where people tend to be more conservative. Some local folks may be open-minded, but others may not be. It's often best to keep your orientation your own business."

Hiking with a partner

There are many opportunities while thru-hiking to experience the benefits of personal growth whether hiking with a partner or hiking solo. The

55

majority of hikers, if they are perceptive and reflective, allow themselves to experience both methods. Of the 2000 milers surveyed, half were single and half married or in another relationship. Although the majority of those in committed relationships hiked with their partners, a number of women did leave them at home and either hiked solo or met up with compatible partners along the Trail.

Author of hiking books and 2000 miler, Karen Berger, has covered thousands of miles of trail with her husband, Dan. She suggests that one of the female hot buttons is surviving a male hiking partner and having the partnership survive the hike. She sent an article she had written for the August '95 issue of Backpacker and outlined six simple things you can do to keep your partner smiling: talk before you walk, agree on a plan, start slowly, stay flexible, give each other space, and communicate.

Karen adds, "to some degree, all hiking partners-whether romantically involved or not-confront physical disparities because one is invariably stronger or faster than the other. While lots of things are negotiable, like wake-up time and camp chores, you can't negotiate differences in physical strength. When partnerships involve men and women, the problem is exacerbated by the fact that strength is at least partly a function of size. A fit 130-pound woman can hike as far and as comfortably as a fit 180-pound man, but she can't reasonably be expected to carry the same amount of weight. Dividing up pack weight by the ability to carry it, rather than by splitting it down the middle, is one of the easiest ways to even the playing field."

Section hiker, Gail Mary Francis, gmf, found that when hiking with a man, people will assume you are a couple which can be good or bad depending on the situation. "My partner and I shared pack weight as well. It took him a while to admit that our weight should not be equal since he was heavier and stronger than me and should carry more weight."

Kelly Winters, Amazin' Grace, went to the Trail to sort things out and needed a lot of time to think. "I chose to hike alone until I figured these things out. I knew if I hiked with others before that time, I could end up putting in a lot of miles, joking and laughing and having camaraderie all the way up the Trail. This would have distracted me from my real purpose in being out there. I needed time to really grow and change. I would not have been self-reliant, and not been out there in the wind and weather solely in charge of my own experience and my own hike. That was a beautiful experience that changed me forever, and I would not trade it for a hike with others. However, after a thousand miles, I was ready to hike with someone else, and grew from that in a different way. Both kinds of experience are valuable."

"In general, I think women are taught that they can't be alone, can't take care of themselves, can't deal with nature, can't be strong. For this reason, I encourage every woman to hike alone for at least part of the trip. You might learn some surprising things about yourself. And you won't learn them any other way."

Lisa Groshong warns that the tiniest personality defect will become hugely magnified during the intense experience of thru-hiking. "I began my hike with an old family friend, and within two months I wanted to murder him. We split up and I hiked with some fantastic women. I would recommend to any woman who wants to hike the trail, go ahead and start alone and within a few weeks you'll meet someone cool. Stay flexible and open to switching partners as your needs and goals and interests change. The Trail is a fluid experience."

" For me, hiking with a partner was essential. I needed the security of company and someone to talk with. I found hiking with a man annoying and dangerous. He had a huge ego and it drove him crazy that I was stronger than he was. He never wanted to take a day off, he acted stupid and obnoxious, he wouldn't talk about his feelings, and he threw tantrums. He wouldn't take a break, even when he was injured. Even now, he has held our common photographs hostage for two years refusing to release them as per our pre-trail agreement because he says he doesn't agree with the way I hiked, even though we split up."

Carolyn Cunningham, Tawanda, suggests that, "If one wants to learn about oneself, then perhaps hiking alone and having to make major decisions alone is the best way to go. But, if one wants to share this experience with a friend or loved one, personal growth may mean a very different thing. A married couple may want to experience what it is like to spend so much time together."

Carolyn started the Trail with another woman, but did not end up finishing together. "We just had too many different ideas about how we wanted to hike. While we started by sharing all of our gear, we ended up completely independent from each other. It got to the point where I would get to town and find a half-empty maildrop box waiting for me at the hostel. It was an awful experience although I learned a lot about myself in the process. In the end it is up to the individual woman to decide what works best for her. I met many couples who decided to break up their intimate relationships after trying to thru-hike. Being with a partner could mean not being able to finish the Trail if one person is not having fun. Being with a group could mean lack of independence, or it could be a relief for an inexperienced hiker who might not otherwise plan a thru-hike."

Like many women who have been brought up in the scouting tradition, Mary Sands, Mama Boots, suggests a buddy system to help partners keep track of each other. Her groups had times of individuality as well as times together. "Plan your day to suit your taste, but let your friends know your feelings."

Section hiker, Pat Hatton of the Mad Hatters, would rather hike with a partner, but that is primarily because she has a great partner in her husband. "If I did not have such a great partner, I would not have hiked the Trail. However, I can certainly understand other female hikers feeling differently; there is plenty of camaraderie on the Trail; one is alone only if one wishes to be."

Hiking with her boyfriend of five years, Lori Kessler, Dr. Daisy G, rejoiced in sharing the marvel and experience of the AT. "The Appalachian Trail was our first home together, and the friends we made were some of the first 'mutual' friendships we had. As a team, we decided on what our goals were-spiritually, physically, from day-to-day-as well as a philosophy for the entire trip. We watched each other grow and change, and developed ever deepening bonds of trust and love as we discovered how our strengths and weaknesses had the power to aid the other."

Kathy Vann has hiked the Trail with different family partners. "My husband and I had over 1600 miles done together, as section hikers, before he died. I finished the Trail two years later, but again in sections. I am re-doing it with my oldest daughter and we have 410 miles to go. We usually hike two weeks at a crack and hope to finish in '99. I feel that the needs, fears, and support of women thru-hikers are certainly different from ours."

Nancy Robinson and her husband finished their 10-year Odyssey by completing the section in Maine. She writes of her observations over the years with thru-hikers. "I admire the thru-hikers for their endurance; I really enjoy those who tough it out in the worst of conditions. The town stays and the drinking hold no interest for me. I like it when they ford swollen streams, endure lightning storms, blowdowns, ice storms; when they reach deep and pull out a bit of courage they never knew existed. I like to see strengths being built, character being developed, sharing and camaraderie." It should be noted, however, that section hikers deal with all the above Trail situations, just spread out over time. Nancy reflects on the special partnership with her husband and best hiking buddy.

Bogey and Slim are our trail names and we hiked the Appalachian Trail over a period of ten years. My husband, Bogey, coaxed me out on this journey. "I'm not a pack mule," I said. But because I love to be with him and I like adventure I gave it a try. When we first set foot on the trail at Pine Grove Furnace State Park the scents of the pine forest, the streams and fallen leaves filled my head. Something in those scents brought back a memory of a time when I was a small child. Although I'd forgotten this place long ago the scents were as vivid as the days when my parents took the family camping nearby. It elicited strong feelings of comfort, like coming home after a long journey. And now add to it I was there with the man who loves me. The romance begins....

Our hike through life as a team began when we were 15 years old. We do almost everything together, but hiking is where we gained individual strengths in our relationship. Friends and family have commented, "What a team!" This was not as noticeable before our hiking. Bogey and I have a unique relationship. Unlike most men, he wants me to be in charge of most things and is not threatened by my strengths. Simply stated, do the job you are best at doing and let the jobs you are not to someone who is. He goes with the flow and I make the current. We consider ourselves best friends. What one lacks the other supplies and we draw strength from one another.

On the Trail we share camp duties, hopes and fears. We share comfort too. When our legs and feet are wracked with pain, we give each other a massage. Just having someone with whom you can be that intimate helps soothe many different kinds of pain. When he wanted to quit, I would massage his spirit and help him to keep going. When I was physically exhausted, he'd carry some of my gear. We've pulled each other up cliffs, eased one another off boulders, carried and dragged, squiggled and slid when necessary. There was a time when he was feeling weak from a cold and said, "I hate this hiking! I've been doing this for you all these years and I hate it!" Can you imagine how bad I felt when he said that? I guess I deserved it. I'd reminded him of the many times I endured a bad cold while hiking and that, if I could do it, he could too. That kind of fired him up a bit. "My colds are worse than yours," he reminded me.

Our relationship has grown stronger since we began hiking the Trail. We do not quarrel over trivial things. Little problems just get in the way of living and we have too little of that left. I no longer expect him to supply my needs or to make me happy. In the beginning I wouldn't have considered going hiking alone but now I do it all the time. All the while we have become more independent and have developed individual strengths which make us stronger as a couple. We love to tent out under the stars and talk about God and His marvelous creations, about us and our family and how great it is to be together. No noise, just the sounds of two hearts fluttering in synch with nature. "It doesn't get any better than this," is our benediction and will be our epitaph. What could be better than being where you love to be with someone you love? The Trail is just an extension of who we are, a synergy of hope and strength.

Many women choose to find a partner before they start their hike, but can also be reassured that they can easily find one once they hit Springer. Kelly Winters, Amazin' Grace, suggests, "Just hike. You will meet all kinds of people, and you'll find one or more who are congenial and whose hiking style matches yours. This is much better than trying to find someone before the trip, especially someone you don't know well. What if one of you wants to hike 25 miles a day following the white blazes and the other one is a 15 mile a day blue blazer? You won't know what your style is until you've been hiking a while. If you keep running into the same person on the Trail and get along well, he/she is probably hiking the same way you are. There are a lot of people on the Trail, so many that hiking alone is more a matter of choice than something you're forced into. It is harder to convince people you do NOT want to hike with them, than to find a partner when you want one."

Kelly's mention of hiking all the white blazes, otherwise known in hiking circles as being a purist, refers to an individual who makes a conscious decision to hike every single white blaze of the Appalachian Trail. This is not a new concept in hiking circles. George Outerbridge, who hiked with Dr. Mary Kilpatrick, the first woman 2000 miler, wrote of their 1930's section hike, "We have done no skipping or shortcutting, but have stuck right to the Trail the whole way...We are certain that we have at no time deviated to any significant extent from the established route. This may seem to some to be merely something in the way of a 'stunt', but we do not look on it in that light. The Appalachian Trail is a real entity, and we felt that if one set out to follow it, he should do just that, and not something 'almost,' but not quite (Hare, pg. 27)."

Many hikers feel it is a matter of personal integrity in being honest with themselves and others that they have really hiked the whole Appalachian Trail and not skipped parts here and there because they were just too tired, lazy, or couldn't be bothered. Although some hikers may need to deviate from their original plans because of a change in life circumstances, illness or injury, they do return and make up the parts they missed. If the pieces are not completed within that same continuous time frame, the hike is considered a section hike rather than a thru-hike. All hikers completing the whole Trail, however long it takes, are called 2000 milers whether it is done in one continuous journey or as many years as it takes to complete.

Lisa Price, The Three Amigos, has a deep respect for the meaning of the 2000 mile patch. She section hiked every year from 1990-1995. "I got to Mahoosuc Notch in April, and spent about two hours trying to get through it. I figure I got about half way before an insurmountable wall sent me backtracking. I remember when I had to face the decision of turning back. I sat dejectedly on a boulder. At the same moment I realized that my period had just started. One of the few times I cried on the Trail!"

"Although it's only a mile, it's a mile I haven't done, so I haven't sent for my patch. For me, hiking the Trail meant hiking ALL the Trail. I really don't care how other hikers approach this. Everybody hikes their own hike. I just know that I wouldn't feel right about wearing that patch yet."

"I've since moved to Maine and will go through the Notch, hopefully this summer. I fractured my kneecap in May and hope it is strong enough by then. It's almost like I'm waiting for some special time (or person?) to complete the Trail with. I know that in the unending phenomena of Trail magic, things will fall into place. If I wind up doing it alone, I know that the shadows that follow me will be four-legged."

Hikers with a more relaxed attitude may skip sections of the Trail as they leapfrog their way north or take a short-cut avoiding some white blazes. This technique is called blue blazing. Some may have to change original plans to fulfill family commitments and jump ahead. Still others grab a lift eliminating whole sections of the Trail by following the "yellow" blaze of the center of the highway.

Following the white blazes is a decision made before you start your thru-hike. It has been said that blue blazing and yellow blazing are like losing your virginity. Once it's gone, you can't get it back. The decision is whether that's important enough to you to take a few minutes, at least, to consider how you want to hike your hike. The decision will be made for you if you don't consider it early enough. The first time your partner or best trail buddy wants to take a side route to avoid a few Trail miles or a mountain without a view, you will have to decide. Are all the months of planning going to hinge on sticking with this individual or will you decide to follow along with your own plan and most likely catch up with them in a couple of days. It's up to you and it pays to think about it before you ever step foot on the Trail.

Melody Blaney, Midnite, '96, advertised in the Trailway News and Lindi Ullyart from South Africa answered her ad. "I had the greatest partner in the world. From her first letter I felt sure we would be compatible. We met the day before our hike began and it was a partnership made in heaven." Melody felt that hiking with Out of Africa enhanced her personal growth and she was made richer by having a partner to share the thru-hiking experience. "For me, the biggest advantage of having a partner was companionship, someone to share the highs, lows, and all the in-betweens, lend a hand when I needed it, provide a shoulder to cry on when the going got tough, and rejoice with me at Katahdin. Safety was another important factor, both in camping, hitchhiking as well as in case of emergency. I think the Trail would be quite lonely going solo." Melody writes free-lance articles about the Trail and, with Lindi, co-authored a book, A Journey of Friendship.

"I feel blessed by my time on the Trail with my significant other," writes Bethann Morgan. "Having to work out the tough times of exhaustion, fear, and frustration helped not only to strengthen our relationship, but it helped me to do some intense soul searching. It was almost as if my partner's support allowed me to step back and take a very serious look at my actions and what drives them. I got a chance to see what I do that gets in the way of growth and quality interaction with other people. I have gained in self-esteem and I know I can hike anywhere and survive and thrive, but I choose to do so with my significant other as it was such an excellent adventure and spiritual growing point."

Section hiker, Martha Manzano, Gypsy, relates an incident she experienced observing a couple in their 50's. "I left the shelter before them and it rained the entire morning. I arrived at the next shelter at noon and the couple came along shortly. I decided to call it quits for the day and stay at the shelter and dry out. The man announced they were hiking another 6 miles. He went to get water and the wife spoke in a low voice, 'I wish we could stay. I wish I could go home. He won't hike on without me, but it's his hike and not mine. He has to do the mileage to get finished in time to return to his job, but I don't like going this fast.' Men don't like to hear it and will usually deny it, but they are obsessed with mileage and speed, the older ones as much as the younger ones. In all fairness, some women are equally obsessed but most not."

Women &Thru-Hiking on the Appalachian Trail

There are women who can hike many men into the dust and have no problem setting the pace and keeping their male partners on their toes. Some hike solo and breeze right by. This mileage mentality game for many women, however, is a killer of relationships and reduces women to tears, injury, and discouragement...sometimes a marriage break-up. Many women do manage to keep up but they pay a price in their enjoyment of their own hike and finding the challenge on their own terms. It makes one wonder about the nature of the relationship off the Trail.

Ginny Owen, Spirit Walker, speaks about freedom and loneliness. "I have done a lot of solo backpacking, and there are a lot of things I really enjoy about it. There is a freedom to it, living totally in the moment, spontaneously. I enjoy sitting quietly under a tree, listening to the silence. I enjoy making my own decisions. I enjoy spending time alone, with me. At the same time it can be lonely. When living life so intensely, it is really good to share it with someone. The joys are doubled, and the trials made a lot easier to bear when they are shared. The AT is a combination of the two even for a solo hiker. The Trail is very crowded, especially in the south. You end up hiking with and around people most of the time. It is very easy to pick up partners, even if only for a few days. In fact, I found it very difficult to find time alone to enjoy the peace of the mountains."

Ginny also warns about how easy it is to get into "groupthink" letting others make all the decisions. She adds, "A lot of the relationships on the Trail are essentially superficial. Everyone is very friendly, but it takes time to make a real friendship. If you keep hiking your own hike, you may end up only spending brief periods with a lot of different people. It can be hard to have any conversations that go beyond the Trail itself. With partners, or longer term hiking friendships, you can reach a depth that makes a hike much better."

This "groupthink" Ginny mentions can be an insidious force that prevents both men and women from getting the most from their hikes. It is often born of fear. While it does create a sense of wonderful camaraderie and security, it also acts as a prevention from getting all that is possible from an extended long distance backpacking trek that may be a once in a lifetime opportunity. Mature hikers appreciate the ramifications a thru-hike can have on one's personal growth. Their younger counterparts often reduce a thru-hike to an extended party tainting this unique adventure in the process.

Ginny further discusses togetherness. "A lot depends on the type and quality of the relationship. My husband and I met on the Trail, so we know we hike well together. Our paces are similar, and consensus is very easily achieved. Our Trail relationship translated very well into our marriage. We both have a pretty good idea of what is important and what isn't. On the Trail, if one half of the partnership wants to hike long days, while the other wants short days, or if one hikes three miles per hour while the other hikes two, or one wants to visit every motel along the Trail while the other wants to 'rough it', there can be some real problems. Frequent compromise is necessary. How well do you handle compromise? One way of dealing with it is to hike separately and only meet at the end of the day, but most couples seem to prefer to hike together. Therein lies the rub. If you hike all day every day together, a thru-hike is more togetherness than most couples experience in a lifetime."

"A lot of couples who do the Trail discover more about themselves and their partner than they had known in many years of living together. This can be good or bad. It helps if you really like each other. Likewise, when hiking alone, it helps if you like yourself, since you spend so much time alone with your own thoughts. It also helps if your relationship is a real partnership. The Trail is too difficult to try to 'carry' a partner. Each must be strong in their own way, able to carry the weight, both physical and emotional, of a thru-hike. If one half is always taking care of the other, they may not have the strength to finish. If you are willing to take turns taking care of the other and being taken care of, it really helps. Everyone has their down days, when it just seems too difficult. That's when a good partner helps. I think most end up changing along the way, but I also think that a good partnership will get better, while a weak one can end up broken."

Jim and Illah Sink, Two Look Slim and Sunflower, married for thirty-five years, agreed to never criticize each other on the Trail and brought their mutual love, respect, faith, patience, and caring to the trials of the Trail experience. Tall, lanky Jim always walked a short distance behind Sunflower to avoid crashes if she stopped suddenly mid-trail. In fact, she stopped so frequently at the beginning that he got two looks.... and his Trailname.

Susan Roquemore, The Dragon Lady, hiked the Trail with David, The Hermit, her husband of thirty years. On their first AT venture she was pretty sure he would be sending her postcards from the edge of Maine about the time she was getting out of Georgia. That made her mad. "You didn't tell me there were mountains on this Trail!" Eventually she looked at a map. "It's not that I am stupid, it's just that I ignore problems like mountains, hunger, thirst, and jungle rot." David sat her down one night and said, "I want to finish this Trail. I want you to finish it with me." They did. Twice.

Susan says that she would not have hiked the Trail once let alone twice if it hadn't been for David. "It's a moot point since he is my life, but the AT was my idea. I was a lousy hiker who grew strong." Susan has taken her Trail expertise to Florida where she has co-authored a book with Joan Hobson on the Florida Trail. About acquiring a Trail partner, Susan's advice is: "Be nice. Partners are like walking sticks; the best ones are found on the Trail."

Kathy Cummins, Fruitcake, who hiked from Georgia to West Virginia in '97 observes, "The partners that did well together were often married to each other or engaged. Those folks seemed to do just fine much more often than not. A frequent reason for leaving the Trail was because the spouse left at home was having a bad time of it. This was usually the wife left at home and not the husband, as was my situation. There were very few people like me, the married woman on the Trail alone. I missed my family, but not painfully. Heck-the conjugal visits were great! And my teenage daughters were proud of me."

Kay Cutshall, The Old Gray Goose, provided some significant topics the hiking half of a couple may want to consider discussing with a loved one before hitting the Trail. The partner at home may not be aware of aspects of Trail life not acceptable off the Trail: hitchhiking to towns to re-supply, going co-ed in a motel room to save money, sharing a tent, sleeping elbow to elbow with the fellows in the shelter, when, if, and how long to schedule visits along the Trail, and what kinds of information can the hiker really wait to hear until she comes home. Goose asks, "Can you really explain Trail life to your old man." Goose considers herself an old fashioned gal who hikes with the blessing of her husband.

Section hiker, Hilary Lang, Weatherwoman, found the perfect hiking partner. "Growler and I were looking for a lot of the same things on the Trail. I met him on Springer Mt. and hiked with him until halfway through the Smokies. He and I rarely hiked together, which was good. We met up for breaks, at good views, at water sources, at night, or just when we wanted to talk. I typically hiked behind him, but if I needed to vent I would be able to catch him. If I wanted more time alone, I'd stop somewhere and let him get farther ahead."

"Even if you start alone, you're never really alone on the Trail," writes Carey Field, Pennsylvania Rose. "You'll meet these great people at the shelter on Springer and you'll all plan to camp together that night. You may walk with one of them. Even if you don't, there will be people waiting for you making sure you get to where you're supposed to be. You can't avoid their concern. Hikers look out for one another. Just use common sense if you're walking alone, and know that everyone in your Trail family will help you if you need it. In my personal opinion, hiking with a permanent partner limits the flexibility and therefore the enjoyment of a hike. You end up trying to please the partner, they try to please you, and your own hikes are put on the back burner." Carey, like all the women, is speaking from personal experience. She met her future husband in Fontana after starting her thru-hike attempt solo.

Kay Cutshall, The Old Gray Goose, describes different sorts of partners. There were partners that she would not see until the end of the day and then would share dinners concocting some good combinations. She would hike together with other partners but not share anything after getting into the shelter. On short hikes a female friend would join Goose on the Trail mostly hiking together and sharing the evening cooking. With all these types of partnerships, which are fairly typical for many thru-hikers, they would discuss the next day's hike and go over the maps. The nature and variety of partnerships is such a fluid entity unless one is in a committed relationship.

A '98 hiker married only 1 1/2 years learned how to deal and cope with problems on the Trail. "My husband doesn't handle certain problems well. His words are, 'I don't do frustration!' So, if a piece of our equipment became faulty, like our tent poles, he would not want to spend a lot of time trying to fix it. He would want to 'Mickey Mouse' it until we could get it fixed professionally. I know this about him, so because of my patience, I was able to deal with these times."

"Men approach a thru-hike, as they do other things in life, as a competition." Sue Freeman, Blueberry, speaks of hiking with her husband and male hikers in general. "They rise in the morning and brag to each other about how they're going to do 'big miles' today. Then we'd find them at the same spot as us at the end of the day having done a typical day, not 'big miles.' I battled with my husband to relax and stop being competitive on the Trail. It's the only thing we fought about. If someone approached us he'd shift into high gear. He didn't like anyone passing him and he'd get mad at me if I didn't speed up, too. Women approached the Trail with the goal of enjoying nature and the company of others. I never saw competitiveness from any woman on the Trail."

Sue also adds that the hike strengthened their relationship. "We joked before the trip that we couldn't carry a gun for protection because one of us would probably shoot the other before the Trail was done. In reality, we enjoyed the time together and now work together every day."

"For my husband and me, sharing pack weight is the only way we accomplished a thru-hike. I don't think I could have carried all that was necessary to do a solo hike. It gave us flexibility to shift weight according to who was in better health or feeling stronger. We routinely shifted items back and forth between us and shared one of many things like the tent, cook stove, pot, fuel, and first aid supplies. We used weight shifting to balance our hiking speed and endurance. This generally meant giving my husband more weight and me the more bulky items to slow him down. Sharing pack weight only works if there is 100% commitment between partners to hike together, otherwise you'll find yourself without some crucial item at some point. For us, commitment wasn't an issue. We were in this together from start to finish, no matter what."

Martha Manzano, Gypsy, suggests that men with longer legs can cover more ground and seem to go faster. "If you begin a thru-hike with such a man or with one who tries to hang back to let you keep up with him, your partnership will probably not last long. You will need to find someone who hikes more at your own pace and will lope happily along way ahead of you." Gypsy hiked with a woman who became very depressed because her first partner was trying to do in excess of 20 miles a day and really pushed her to keep up.

"She and I hiked very well together doing 8-10 mile days except that after a while our styles clashed. I'm a morning person and hate to hike more than a few miles after lunch while she liked to sleep late and seemed to get a burst of energy around 3 or 4 p.m. You will probably have an assortment of hiking partners for a thru-hike so keep it in the back of your mind if you start with someone so you won't be devastated if it doesn't work out."

"Expect at least some of the male thru-hikers to try to turn the hike into a competition," warns Dania Egedi, Lightweight. "How you handle this depends on you. I usually prefer to leave them in my dust, even if it means collapsing along the Trail a quarter mile past where they did. Other times, I just waved them on by. Who really cares who gets to the top of the hill first!"

Sherri Swartz, Sunrise, was eager to address the special problems of petite women. She is 5'1" with a 26" inseam and weighs 115 pounds. "Some short women still hike really fast and have no problem keeping up with the 'guys', but I had a hard time keeping up with anyone. I realized I was at a disadvantage in two ways. I had to take about 20% more steps per mile than a 6 ft. man, and my pack weight was always a greater percentage of my body weight that it would be on a larger person. Fortunately, I was hiking with my husband, so I shared gear with him and he was able to take a greater amount of our pack weight."

"For small women hiking alone, I would just recommend to be ruthless in looking at the weight of everything in your pack. If you're buying gear for the hike, look into children's or women's size sleeping bag and clothes. Why carry a 6' long sleeping bag when you're only 5' tall? You can also get by with a smaller tent than most people without getting claustrophobic."

"It was discouraging on my hike to watch others hike 20+ mile days and still have time to savor the views or relax at the shelter in the evening. The miles just never came easy to me. If I wanted to keep up with a group that was going to a certain place that day, I would have to get up early and leave early and would usually get there after they had all set up camp. For awhile I felt like a wimpy hiker, until I did the math and realized that when I did a 16 mile day with a 35 pound pack, it was equivalent to a 6 ft 180 pound guy doing a 20 mile day with a 55 pound pack. It also helped when I caught up to a group of women, after seeing no women for several weeks, and realized that their daily mileage was similar to mine."

"I would also recommend that small women not plan too ambitious a schedule or too limited a time frame for their hike. If you turn out to be a fast hiker, no problem. But if your short legs slow you down, you won't have to feel as rushed. I took about 6 1/2 months for my hike and am glad I didn't have to go any faster." Sherri and her husband were married for almost five years before they started their thru-hike. "I wouldn't really recommend it for a honeymoon or for a relationship where there is not total commitment."

Donna Horn, '78, sees many advantages hiking solo but one of the major advantages of hiking with a partner is that it is nice to share the adventure with someone you care about. If you always need company, you have someone with you. She suggests that, "Before hiking with a partner, whether a friend, spouse, or significant other, you need to clarify your goals: are you on the AT to hike together, or are you each on a hike to get to Maine? That translates into what happens when one is sick, injured, or sick of hiking and can't or doesn't want to continue hiking. Discussing alternatives to the what ifs BEFORE starting on the hike will make contingency planning a lot easier. If one gets off, does the other automatically get off, too, or does the other person continue on?"

Kathy Kelly Borowski, '89, warns, "If you are not as committed to the partnership or trip, you may be left unprepared Communicate if things

70

are not working out. I think you will do better finding someone with your pace and interest in traveling on the same schedule once you get started. My partner left with little explanation and then told others it was my fault. Guess she could not take responsibility for her own decision. She never talked to me about the problems she was having. Then I felt guilty for a while, that I had actually done something wrong. Finally, the group I was hiking with reminded me I was still on the Trail and she was not."

Is it possible to be intimate on the Trail?

Sarah Dixon thinks that women are impacted more by the relationships they make on the AT than are the men. She was 18 when she attempted a thru-hike in '88. "I think there is a sense of accomplishment of sorts for both sexes. But guys want to put the miles behind them and the girls want to see them at the shelters at night. The guys want a good spot in the shelter and the girls want the spot next to the guy. Not that we're all hungry for sex or a relationship, we just value that time and want to feel like we're special to someone."

"Although I hiked solo," writes Dania Egedi, Lightweight, "I hiked with a number of women who were hiking with their partners. By far their biggest complaint was that their partners preferred to hang around 'with the guys.' That made it difficult to be intimate, sexually or otherwise, with any regularity. Many were very tired of having so many other people around on what they thought would be a time where they and their partner would be mainly interdependent on each other. Most didn't feel like they could say much because their partner was enjoying the company of their 'newfound friends.' Many resented it and it often became a bone of contention further down the Trail."

"Yes, definitely" writes T. Whittaker, Luna. "I met my husband on the Trail, got married on the Trail after the hike, and had my honeymoon on the Trail. We very rarely slept in shelters and found our tent or bedroll under the stars very romantic. We camped on lonely mountaintops and occasionally in more private places. We also hiked with many friends and had a great balance with time spent alone and time with others. Get creative and be open. The cleanliness thing got a bit much after a while but after a town stop or shower, we would fall in love all over again."

"Trail conditions are wonderful for intimacy," adds Sue Freeman, Blueberry. "What better situation than to make love surrounded by nature? My husband and I often headed off the Trail to a secluded hollow to share intimate moments. Or, we would sometimes choose to tent alone in the woods for privacy at night. Shelters or tents near others are not the appropriate place. Most nights we enjoyed the company of others and were usually too tired from the day's hike to consider anything but sleep anyway." Others report that often the interest and the energy were just not there.

Vicki McMahan writes, "Shhhhh..... Intimacy has its place on the Trail. Just remember, its place is in private, respect your fellow hikers, and don't make them listen! A shelter is not the place for this, a tent is a must, or even a quiet secluded place that you find during the day. Just keep the volume on mute! This activity might be best suited after a trip into town or a nice swim somewhere where you can get rid of that trail odor. Baby wipes work great for clean up after and you don't have to leave the warm tent!"

A young solo hiker addresses the question of sex on the Trail. "Since I was alone, and there are not a lot of solo women out there, I often had lonely guys ask, how about it? I was not interested, for various reasons, number one being that I didn't go on the trip to meet guys. Even if you are interested, after a day of hiking, you will probably be too tired! If you want casual sex, I'm sure you could find it, but the women who indulged in it seemed to get distracted from whatever their original mission was in being out there. They got caught up in all the relationship baggage that most people go to the Trail to take a break from. Everyone on the Trail is in a time of change; everyone's a rolling stone. It's a good place to make lifelong friends, but I wouldn't advise looking for a serious sexual relationship there. If you are hiking with your partner, well, then this stuff doesn't apply; have fun!"

Susan Roquemore, The Dragon Lady, suggests, "Practice being a little quiet and you can do anything you do at home and chances are you will be going to a motel once a week anyway." She acknowledges the fact that men are attracted to women! "There are many jokes on the Trail about 'a little trail romance'. The reason these 'jokes' abound is that the people involved are not discreet, are not polite, and generally annoy their shelter-mates with their love-throes. That behavior isn't cool. Frankly, nobody really cares who sleeps with whom and it isn't anybody's business. Don't get drunk, shack up in town, then expect respect on the Trail where gossip abounds."

Susan also adds a bit of mature advice. "Don't come out on the Appalachian Trail looking for a lover: these guys are hiking 20 mile days and their virility comes second to a hot pot of ramen noodles. By the same token, if you choose to be a thru-hiker yourself, the men will protect you as if you were golden. You will find that chivalry, not to be confused with chauvinism, is not dead. If you do decide to have a romance, don't consider it any more than a passing fancy. Picking you out of a swollen stream and hugging you does not constitute true love."

Kelly Winters, Amazin' Grace, '96 says, "It can be weird when you're packed in with one or two or even a bunch of lonely guys who haven't seen a woman in a while. They get into a real 'locker-room' conversation about women or one guy will decide that he's walked the Trail just to meet you. You're his soulmate, and you don't even know it! Act like a sister/aunt/mother/grandmother (depending on your age), and they will eventually treat you like one. Don't feel that you have to smile, appease the guys, or otherwise put up with this stuff. You don't. You're hiking the Trail for your own reasons, not to provide companionship or services to lonely guys. If a guy repeatedly hassles you and is clueless even when you tell him off, just get out of sync with him. Hike a day ahead or a day behind. This effectively puts him in a kind of alternate universe, and you'll never see him again. End of problem."

Another hiker laments bringing her significant other into the trail environment. "My significant other visited while I was hiking, and the only way to be intimate is to get a hotel room. Take a shower. We hiked together twice, and only once stayed in a town. I thought hiking together would be great because I'd get to show off the trail experience, but in reality it was bringing an outsider into something they absolutely couldn't grasp in such a short time, It was stressful and we never had sex because I hadn't had a shower in weeks. We were in Connecticut and couldn't afford to stay anywhere. Bad, bad planning. Very disappointing visit."

Dania Egedi, Lightweight, suggests that unattached females are often hit on. "How you handle this depends on your particular disposition. Remember that you are making your reputation. By Virginia, most women have either formed a relationship with someone, or the word is out that they aren't interested."

Hiking Solo

Verna Soule, Gran'ma Soule, loves the freedom of hiking solo, sitting beside a stream and relaxing or on a mountain ledge and just looking. Like many hikers, she has also hiked with partners and with groups.

"One of my greatest joys of my experience hiking from Georgia to West Virginia was feeling capable and independent. I did camp alone sometimes, and enjoyed this freedom. I am glad I chose to hike alone. I was comfortable and refused to be made to feel afraid," states Kathy Cummins, Fruitcake.

Kristen Lincoln met a lot of people hiking solo and felt she could do whatever she wanted to do whenever she wanted and didn't have to wait for others. DJ McCulloch states that all the doors are open when solo hiking. Other women also affirmed the solo thru-hiking experience as the only way for them.

"The times I learned the most about myself was when I was hiking alone." Nancy Marth, Geo, feels that a lot of her new knowledge came from having to use her own physical strength and ingenuity to get her through difficult situations. "Some of my knowledge came from the fact that I didn't have someone waiting for me at the shelter or up around the next bend. Many people when faced with this loneliness think, 'OK, what do I do now?' But that's the time when you learn you CAN handle camping solo, and you CAN get over those slippery rocks, or you CAN deal with not having anyone to talk to. You just learn how, and when you learn how, you learn to enjoy your own time and you gain confidence in yourself. It may seem lonely at times, but you'll be glad you spent at least part of the Trail hiking solo."

Dania Egedi, Lightweight, expresses the advantages of a woman solo thru-hiking in terms of freedom.

Freedom to make your own decisions without having to justify (or even mention) them to someone.

Freedom to make or break friendships without regard to how much your significant other likes the person.

Freedom to be sick or healthy on any given day.

Freedom to talk about whatever without regards to how it will effect your relationship with your significant other.

You meet more people.

Regina Erskine, Whispering Pine, thru-hiked in '97. "I found mostly advantages to my solo thru-hike. I only needed to worry about me. I could stop when I wanted, hike on when I wanted at whatever pace I wanted, take a day off, eat and sleep when I wanted. I didn't feel that I was in danger because I was by myself and a woman. If for some reason I felt I needed someone nearby, I could often seek out a fellow thru-hiker."

Kathy Kelly Borowski, '89, states the advantages of hiking solo. "You can make your own schedules. Come and go as you please. You are only responsible for you. You have time alone with yourself to get your head straight, set new goals, and take a look at your life."

From the Trail in '98, Melissa Sumpter, Selky, writes, "I wouldn't have it any other way. We fight all battles alone. Walking into this adventure as a solo hiker was one of the best parts of my trip. My world was open to my desires. I didn't have to consider anyone else when planning. There was no coordinating maildrops and mileage. It was just me and my pack open to the endless possibilities of the Trail. I was free to meet people as they came my way, free to hike my own hike whether it meant walking alone or changing groups daily. I was free to decide. Was there fear in that freedom? No! Only beauty. I wasn't afraid of the people I might meet or the accidents I might have. There's no time for such worries when you're busy enjoying the beauty of life."

Jeanne Spellman, through an unusual combination of

circumstances, spent more than six weeks alone on the AT seeing people only on weekends. "It was a wonderful life-changing experience. I had some times when I was very frightened, but rarely because I thought there was danger from other people or animals. I was afraid when I broke my foot alone, but I dealt with it successfully. I was afraid when I spent two days in an open shelter during a howling snowstorm, but I also dealt with it successfully. I am so proud of what I was able to do by myself, that it gave me the courage to do many other things that I was afraid of in the 'real world', like negotiating salary increases and taking leadership roles. I believe it is important to know my fears, be able to assess the real risk, and go forward or change plans accordingly."

Donna Savluk, Ward's Girl, always starts out section hiking alone. "The main advantage is that you are completely flexible. You can decide to hang around a shelter all day in the rain, or do a 20+ miler, to have a glass of wine with dinner. Hiking with a partner can and probably would make these things difficult. It is always possible to speed up or slow down to get away from anyone who is annoying you on the Trail. You also gain a greater sense of responsibility for yourself, by being 'out there' alone."

Beverly Hugo, Maine Rose, very briefly, perhaps for five minutes, entertained the notion of hooking up with a partner before her hike. "I spoke to a man in another state who had advertised in the Trailway News and he had all sorts of ideas about sharing packweight and how he thought things should be done. After that one conversation, I knew there would be no option for me other than hiking solo. This decision was made with a clear and perceptive understanding of my temperament and how I might react to having to compromise on every little issue...where to have lunch, where to camp, when to stop, how long to stay in town...the possible compromises seemed endless and something that I was not willing to make. So for 90% of my hike, I went solo making every last decision on my own."

"Being independent to begin with, I still felt it was an amazingly empowering experience to confront so many difficult situations, some even dangerous, and come out safely and stronger for having done it on my own without the help of another person. That was important to me but might not be an issue for many women whose presence on the Trail, in whatever capacity, fulfills whatever their objectives might be. Tenting alone in the woods miles from a shelter and any other hiker was an experience I would not have anticipated before the hike. It became a reality in Virginia, and after that, I actually found myself seeking out the opportunities to repeat those solitary nights in my own company."

"I thoroughly enjoyed the camaraderie of the shelters particularly in the first months of the hike. As the hike progressed I became more one with myself, something that would not have been possible with a partner. I never considered I would need someone to get me out of a jam or to keep me company. The few times I ended up hiking with friends it was fun and companionable. I would not trade those experiences for anything, but I am satisfied and happy that I hiked most of the time alone and did it my way."

Occasionally an experienced woman, used to hiking confidently with a partner or small group, will scoff at the myriad of safety concerns expressed by novice women contemplating long distance hikes. Survey results indicated that 56% of 2000 milers hiked less than 25% of the Trail solo. Many of these hikers also noted that they never hiked even one day solo or spent a night alone in the woods. While it is true that each individual must hike every step on her own, when a woman is hiking solo, she draws completely from her own inner resources. Facing the challenge of sudden lightning storms on an open ridge, ascending that steep section of Wildcat, tenting in the woods far from a shelter, or spending many hours on a regular basis without human contact especially at night, even when it is by choice, is an experience that someone who has never hiked alone does not always understand.

Christine Shaw, Firefly, '96, was 20 years old when she started her solo thru-hike. "For the first four months of my hike, I only met two other solo female hikers, and they were also my age or younger. I never considered the AT in any other way. I knew I had to stand alone. That was part of the whole experience. I couldn't depend on anyone else to get me to Maine, and I had to learn that every day. Many of the women I met looked forward to future hikes when they would go solo. I met a lot of women who had grown up, gone to college, been married for quite some time, and never really been alone. This trip was like a new freedom for them. It opened up an entirely new place in their soul for exploration. It is very hard to stand alone when you have never been that way before. It is also extremely rewarding. No matter what everyone else around you says, I hope that each woman reading this gets a chance to stand alone, and depend only on yourself. You will learn so much."

Melody Blaney, Midnite, echoed similar sentiments. "I feel the biggest benefit is the courage it takes to make the decision to attempt a thru-hike, especially for women who are settled into a comfortable lifestyle in their 30's and 40's. Most women make major life decisions in their life much earlier, after high school or college. Attempting a thru-hike builds a great amount of self-confidence in being able to handle and deal with anything that the Trail puts in front of you."

Ginny Owen, Spirit Walker, spent more time alone on her first thru-hike in '88 hiking solo but often with others. She notes there were fewer hikers on the Trail especially women than on her second hike. In '92 she teamed up with a partner, future husband Jim, and hiked with him for 1500 miles. She was rarely alone, there were many more hikers including women especially women going solo.

Anne Mausolff, The Green Mountaineer, reminds us that aloneness is not necessarily lonely. A woman can go at her own pace, start and stop as it pleases her, and be quietly with herself for a change. A woman has to know her personal ratio of "aloneness vs. company."

Relationships regardless of age and gender

All women hikers speak with enthusiasm about the warmth, support, and love within the thru-hiking community regardless of age and gender. Susan Roquemore, the Dragon Lady, with her usual humor writes, "Seriously, the whole generation gap thing is gone forever and some of your best friends will be twenty-something males and old coots who might just happen to be Catholic priests in Mufti. Attitudes change and nothing bothers you too much except pettiness and squabbles. I haven't been able to abide silly arguments since 1995."

One of her most treasured moments was when a young barrister from England woke her while she was sleeping with her husband Dave in the big bed in the Blue Blaze Hostel. He said, "Dragon Lady, I've just brewed some sassafras tea with honey...will you wake up and tell me whether it tastes right?" "I did-it did, and I slept nicely knowing I had such friends."

Beverly Hugo, Maine Rose, adds, "For six months I marveled at this wonderful opportunity to be an 'equal' with so many young men and women who could be my own children. I have a feeling many middle aged women hikers have enjoyed these easy parent-like relationships. On more than one occasion a power hiker, usually a young man, would hang back and move along at my 'breakneck' pace chatting amiably about all sorts of philosophical ideas, a treat and a nurturing experience for both of us."

"The day I hiked through Mahoosuc Notch, it took me over six hours to hike 2.8 miles from Full Goose Shelter to the campsite on the other side. I was so pleased with myself. The day was bright and sunny. I set up my tent and aired my sleeping bag on a line in the little campsite ready to tackle South Arm in the morning when I was refreshed. It is important to have a keen sense of your abilities and limitations and this was one of the many times I chose to stop before total exhaustion set in."

"Three young 25+ year old male hikers appeared looking trail worn but confident, self-assured, and ready to tackle the last stretch before the shelter. They had started their day at a distance far before where I had started and would finish beyond me. As an overweight hiker, getting in the miles was always a bit of a struggle while these young guys seemed to breeze right along. I had never met them so was delighted to pass a few minutes finding out about their thru-hikes. They were a pleasure and I was happy meeting new hikers even in Maine. It was only later when I told someone what nice guys they were that I found out all three had horrible reputations for gross disgusting conversation, more for shock value than anything else. It was then that I realized I wasn't being treated as an equal after all.... but as their mother!"

Women often express the concept of family and that their fellow hikers are like brothers and sisters. Kelly Winters, Amazin' Grace, was at a shelter when a local drunk showed up at the campsite and started paying too much attention to her. He decided he had urgent business elsewhere when two male hikers claimed that one was her husband and the other her brother!

Sarah Dixon discusses Trail relationships. "I saw a couple of marriages/significant relationships topple while hiking both years. The Trail is so powerful and yields things most aren't expecting. Not everyone wants or needs or finds the same thing while hiking. I found everything is so on the surface. You make friends almost immediately; you fall in love knowing little or nothing of that person. You live for right now with the people you meet because they may hike away from you tomorrow."

Joyce Johnson, Pilgrim's Progress, usually camped in her tent, but the times she was in a shelter or a hostel with men were ok, if you don't mind the usual male noises. "One time, two men, a father and a son, 68 and 45, probably saved my life. I came into a shelter late, almost dark after walking in rain all day and my gear was wet from the previous rainy night. While trying to get my stove lit for something to drink, I began to shiver violently. They immediately took over putting out my sleeping bag and made me go behind the shelter to get into some dry clothes. They made me get into my bag and brought me hot tea. Such service! We remain friends to this day. They were from Ohio and came to Illinois to visit my family and me after I got home. We did things for each other. That's what hikers and friends do."

Animal Encounters

Most thru-hikers agree that they do not see as much wildlife or as many critters as they would like. If you are the first woman up and out in the morning, you will find yourself using your hiking stick to break through the cobwebs created throughout the night so you don't get them in your face and mouth. Late risers will never feel the joy of being the first hiker on the Trail on that day from that spot. Early risers may also benefit from wildlife sightings not seen later in the day. A mass of hikers traipsing through the woods chattering and clicking their hiking sticks gives notice to the animals to seek further depth in the forest.

Women &Thru-Hiking on the Appalachian Trail

Carol Donaldson, Coosa, section hiker and very active in her Georgia hiking group, feels that encountering animals in their natural habitat is so rare for anyone that it is a time of wonder and joy. "I remember finding a tree full of inchworms all hanging by their 'threads' and sitting on a downed tree with an inch worm on my fingers singing 'inch worm, inch worm, measuring the marigolds'." She recalls seeing the footprint of a bear that never did appear and the vole that jumped over a rock and landed on her chest as she was sleeping under the stars. She remembers the time she climbed up and around some rocks and came face to face with a young owl and the birds that kept singing as she passed within a few feet making her feel as if she was an accepted part of nature.

A '98 hiker got a Brown Recluse bite so upped her mileage and got to town as fast as possible. All hikers allergic to bees need to take special precautions and carry an epi-pen. Occasionally one finds a Ziploc bag weighed down with a rock in the middle of the Trail and with a note inside warning of bees or wasps ahead.

Susanne Wright Ashland had to jump out of the way of a running moose! Susanne warns that small animals that appear to be friendly should be avoided. Shouting or throwing small stones or sticks to scare them away and not hit them usually works. Rabid animals seem to be on the increase in Maine.

Joyce Johnson, Pilgrim's Progress, met a large, male black bear at Peck's Corner Shelter in the Smokey Mts. "I had just gotten to the shelter, saw the bear, and got inside. There was no chain or lock on the gate, but I tied it with a rope. He stuck his head in a large hole in the fence, but after a while, left. I did not cook that night, as I thought the smell of food might bring him back. He was the size of a yearling steer calf, about 400-500 pounds, very aggressive and probably hungry!" Many women, disappointed for sure, never even see a bear their entire thru-hike.

On Sue, White Glove, Kenn's, first thru-hike, a bear came down out of a tree about 70 feet away. "All I could think about was getting his picture! My dad thought the bear might be a threat to us and he started swinging his hiking pole around making all kinds of noises hoping to scare the bear away. It worked and I didn't get a picture. On my attempted thru-

81

hike with my husband, we saw a yearling not too far from us and we did get a picture." Don't ever place yourself between a mother bear and her cubs.

Women often ask if they have more to fear from bears during their periods. An article in Backpacker magazine suggests otherwise. "Steven P. French, noted bear expert, says there has been only one documented bear attack on a menstruating woman in North America, and the investigating team concluded that 'menstruation did not appear to have played a major role.' The myth is probably due to media hysteria. As French writes in "Bites and Injuries Inflicted by Mammals," a chapter from the book Wilderness Medicine (edited by Paul Auerbach, M.D.): 'that menstruation may be a precipitating factor on attacks or predation has unfortunately become solidly ingrained into popular myth'." The case referred to involved a grizzly bear in a western state. There are no cases reported of bear attacks on menstruating women on the Appalachian Trail.

Section hiker Connie Cabe, Muddy, asks, "What would the Trail be like without the funny stories about the mice? I had one sitting in my coffee cup! My fault, I shouldn't have left it out." Kelly Winters, Amazin' Grace, feels you get used to the mice after a while. "They're more an annoyance and health hazard than anything. Don't ever leave food in your pack at night, or they will chew through it to get to the goodies. In shelters, sleep with your head toward the shelter entrance, not toward the wall. Mice tend to stay close to the wall, so sleeping with your head against the back wall or in a corner is asking for trouble." Mice droppings are also responsible for the hanta virus. Withhold that domestic urge, and don't sweep out the shelter stirring up bacteria filled dust and droppings. And if you really hate mice, stick with your tent.

Beverly Hugo, Maine Rose, had an unexpected reaction when seeing so many cows on the Trail. "I spent an idealistic 11 years in Israel in my 20's and 30's, have dual citizenship, and was a kibbutz member milking cows and raising calves. I felt euphoric when I was able to get close to the cows and talked to them as I passed." Many hikers, however, have never been close to a cow and their size, proximity, and numbers in some areas of the Trail can be a cause of anxiety or even fear.

Rosie had an unusual experience on a ridge outside of Pearisburg.

"I was walking along in my usual solo reverie high on a Virginia ridge with glorious ferns spread out to either side. I managed to pry my eyes off the ground where they were usually planted and saw a big bird standing in front of me. It was so absurd I could only chuckle to myself while I took a picture and clucked trying to encourage it to move away. It didn't, so I walked around through the ferns and got another picture from the other side. I was still laughing to myself as I hustled on to the next shelter eager to add what I thought would be a unique entry in the Trail register. It wasn't. Others before me had seen the big bird and were jokingly debating whether it was an emu or an ostrich listing the characteristics of each and even suggesting that it was Elvis re-incarnated. It was an emu and the picture, with a white blaze on a tree in the background, never fails to get a laugh at my slide shows."

Amanda Henck had a snake encounter while hiking with her grandad. "When Pops and I were hiking, we came across a diamond-back rattler sitting all coiled up on the side of the Trail. He wouldn't strike at our hiking sticks, so Pops just flipped him over and he slithered away. I don't know what I would have done had I been alone.... I almost climbed a tree!" Amanda, still a teenager, says that no one in her immediate family is obsessed with nature like she is. "They love hiking, as long as home or an AMC (Appalachian Mountain Club) full-service hut is the destination."

KC Felton has had several snake encounters. "The first time it was a rattlesnake in the middle of the Trail. We could not go around it so tried to get it to move. It took us 45 minutes of prodding but it finally moved far enough out of the Trail for us to pass. Please do not kill snakes. The next encounter was with a big 4 ft. long black snake which grew to at least 6 ft. by the time we got home."

Admire snakes including copperheads and rattlers, grass snakes and black snakes. Watch them for a bit, give them distance, and move on. Don't go sticking your hands in rocky crevices. Use a stick to part the grass in overgrown areas. Don't forget that the forest is their home and you are privileged to share it with them for a short period.

The one animal, other than man, that is the cause of most fears for women on the Trail, is the dog; not a non-existent wild dog rampaging

83

through the forest but sweet little old poochie whose owner swears he won't bite. Dogs on roads near the Trail can also be a cause of concern and great anxiety. More women take pepper spray on the Trail out of fear of dog attack than for any other reason.

Debbie Emerson, Dogmother, warns, "Please train your dog before you take one on a thru-hike. Train them to use a leash, to obey commands, and to wear a backpack. It is irresponsible to take an untrained dog on the Trail. Check with your vet to make sure your dog is healthy enough to make the trip and be aware that if your dog needs medical attention or gets hurt that you may have to leave the Trail. Dogs cannot be asked if they want to do this hike so you have to be sure that you are prepared for getting off the Trail if they are unhappy. Don't put superglue on their pads unless you check with your vet, and don't overpack their backpack. Carry enough water for them and check with vets along the Trail. Don't take them for protection. You can use other things for that."

Section hiker, Lisa Price, The Three Amigos, hiked with different dogs on her various hikes and often with two. "Each dog had its own style on the Trail. Kliban liked to trot ahead and sit down, checking out the trail ahead while keeping me in sight. Maude walked behind me. So in a way those two dogs kept me between them. Both slept in my little tent, a clip flashlight, with me. I had one of my roughest nights on the Trail after a day hiker gave the dogs some deviled eggs - the intensity of the dog farts was truly astounding! Mitch walked behind me, but with him it was hiding. He'd been an abuse case at the pound and he was very shy. Sara alternated between walking with Mitch and walking just in front of us."

"I know that many people are against dogs on the Trail, and I can see why. I don't profess to be a dog expert but there are some simple things dog owners must do to be canine ambassadors - treat your dog's waste as you do your own - bury it. Make sure your dog knows the word 'No' and comes to you when called without exception. Ask before you bring it into a shelter with others. Don't let your dog beg for food. Carry parachute cord; it's light and makes a great leash for roadwalks and towns. Keep your dog well fed and healthy. Your dog should be wearing a tag with the name, phone number and address of a contact person from home in case it gets lost. Although I miss my original amigos (Kliban has also since passed away) I feel that the months on the Trail were the times of their lives. I wouldn't trade it for anything."

Rachel Dubois, Solophile, responsibly thru-hiked in '97 with her dog Micah.

I put a lot of thought into my decision to hike with my dog. I actually have three dogs, but Micah was the only one I felt capable of handling the Trail, and he came through beautifully. I did a lot of homework before I hit the Trail with him. I read everything I could get my hands on about hiking with dogs, I wrote to veterinarians who had done long-distance hiking with dogs, and I talked to previous thru-hikers that had traveled with dogs. I also did physical conditioning for Micah as well as myself. We hiked during the week and weekends leading up to our departure date. We both carried fully loaded packs and I hiked with him on pavement to try and condition his paws.

All of my preparations wouldn't have mattered for anything though if I hadn't had a dog that was physically up to doing the Trail and who loved to hike. I was lucky. Micah was always excited to have his pack put on and to head up the Trail. He was an extremely agile, athletic, and brave-hearted animal. Not all dogs have these qualities, and I'm sure the Trail would be a much more difficult task for them. My number one concern during my hike was the health of my dog. His comfort and well being came before mine always. Micah was the first to eat, the first to drink water, and his health dictated our mileage and our pace. It was the least I could do for the animal that was willing to accompany me on a journey filled with exhaustion and discomfort all because he loved me. I was constantly monitoring his condition. I must have gotten him weighed at least six times while on the Trail to see how he was holding his weight. During the summer heat, we only hiked early morning and late afternoon and I took breaks every hour to let him cool off and rest. If we made ten miles that day, so be it, but my dog was going to stay healthy no matter what.

As soon as he stopped enjoying the hike, I had promised myself that I would send him home. Lucky for me, that day never dawned. Micah was very well behaved. He did not approach strangers, he was protective of me and our gear, and would step off the Trail when others approached and let them pass. Once he had his pack on and was 'working' he would not leave the Trail to chase animals. I kept Micah on a leash at night, mostly to protect him from encounters with skunks, bears, and other animals. We slept in our tent 90% of the time because I didn't want him to intrude upon other hikers or affect their hike in a negative way. When we got to towns, I had to adjust my plans accordingly. Many places did not allow dogs, but I knew to expect that beforehand and adjusted my expectations. When I did hear of an establishment that accepted dogs, I made sure to stay there. I let them know that was why I chose their business and how much I appreciated it.

If I had my hike to do over again, I would still take Micah. He was a lot of extra work, but he was also my best friend and a devoted hiking companion who never complained. Micah gave me a sense of confidence throughout the Trail. I don't know that I could have completed the entire trail without him. He was protective enough to make me feel safe at all times, and yet he made wonderful friendships of his own with other hikers. Micah was an integral part of my hike and the bond that we forged between us after having hiked the Trail is something that will last us a lifetime. Clearly, Solophile sets the standard for responsible dog stewardship on the Appalachian Trail.

Ginny Owen, Spirit Walker, has not thru-hiked with a dog but has experienced two thru-hikes and observed much of the downside of hiking with one. "Not everyone loves dogs, and many hikers are actively scared of dogs. Others just don't like to share shelters and hostels with animals that are likely to get rain and mud on their gear. While many hikers will welcome you and your animal, if you don't pay attention to what it is doing and it gets into the other hikers' gear, beds, and food, you won't be very welcome."

Ginny continues. "Dogs are not welcome in a lot of hostels and motels. This limits your options. They are not allowed in the Smokies or Baxter State Park so arrangements must be made to take care of them while you hike there. What happens if your dog gets caught up with a skunk, a bear, or decides to go chase a deer? A lot of dogs get lost on the Trail or found and taken home by someone else. It is difficult to figure energy needs; a dog's are even harder to figure out. They don't handle the heat and dry conditions well. I've seen some very skinny and exhausted dogs. Many have very sore paws from the rocks and long miles."

"It will change your hike as you have to keep in mind what is good for the dog as well as what is good for you. Do you have a family member who can come pick up the dog if he/she gets hurt or just tired of hiking? If you do bring a dog, bring a tent and don't count on staying in the shelters much, if at all. Your dog must be trained to stay away from hikers unless invited to approach, not to beg, not to drink from or pee in springs, to stay off gear, to stay very close to the owner, to not fight with other dogs, and stay away from wildlife. Hiking with a dog adds a lot of concerns that will change the nature of the thru-hike. It's like hiking with a child. Fewer complaints, perhaps, but a responsibility nonetheless."

As one woman wrote, "I don't recommend hiking with a dog unless you are blind." More than one woman has been embarrassingly sniffed one too many times to appreciate a dog on the Trail. Women have had to defend themselves from attack with their hiking sticks while the dog's owner has stood nonchalantly by saying, "Oh, he won't hurt you." Dogs off the leash tear up the Trail barking and bearing their teeth while owners take their time meandering up behind them. Most hikers have enough concerns about their personal safety without worrying about getting bitten and having their hike altered by a dog with an inconsiderate owner.

Special health conditions and considerations

Some women have specific health conditions and considerations, and although this may hamper their progress, it doesn't keep them from taking to the woods. Several section hikers with diabetes check their blood a couple of times a day and pay special attention to their dietary needs. Others have an intense fear of heights and work to overcome this.

Section hiker, Connie Cabe, Muddy, had Graves disease (hyperthyroidism) and is now on synthetic thyroid every day. "My energy levels are not what they used to be prior to this condition and it is

87

sometimes frustrating. Also, my metabolism seems to be slower."

Kathy Kelly Borowski started experiencing migraine headaches four years before her thru-hike. "When I put myself in very stressful conditions on the Trail, I would get a migraine. I tried to rest and abort it. Again, my desire to hike the Trail would not let me give up due to a headache. This desire was always greater than any anxiety, pain, or panic experienced while hiking."

"I suffer from irritable bowel syndrome (IBS)," writes a young woman. "I found that thru-hiking was one of the few times in my life when I was not affected by my condition. The exercise and state of mind that I experienced on the Trail was one of the best things for me. IBS is a horrible condition because your digestive system is constantly irregular. This could be in the form of constipation, diarrhea, or just plain pain. On the Trail, though, I can't remember ever having a fit. I attribute a lot of this to my state of mind. I was so peaceful and carefree it was difficult for my system to feel stressed out."

Jean Arthur, now retired, hikes at least one day a week after completing her nine year section hike. "Hiking and exercise have caused me to lose weight, helped my blood pressure, and kept me from becoming crippled with arthritis. I have developed strength, muscles, and stamina."

On the Trail in '98, a woman shares her diagnosis at 17 with a rare illness called sarcoidosis. "I spent much of my senior year on crutches. I was like an old woman, often holding my mother's arm for support. When I went into remission my father asked me to go hiking with him. One hike changed my life. I started hiking every weekend. I became young again. The timid old woman was gone. I began to do all the things I had been afraid to even dream of. Now I am face to face with my biggest dream. The AT white blazes have been dancing in my head since my first hike. Now I have the opportunity to see them all."

A section hiker writes, "All my life I had severe asthma which kept me from doing anything strenuous. I was allergic to cats, bacteria, and house dust, and my parents smoked. I took up the habit and then in 1981, with the Lord's help, gave up cigarettes. After two years I was able to live and breathe for the first time in my life. I live with gusto now, trying to capture the lost adventures of youth. I am driven. When father death calls my name he'd better know how to run 'cause he's gonna have to catch me." This former smoker became a 2000 miler in '98.

A woman suffering from chronic fatigue syndrome, CFS, found some help so she could continue her hiking trips. "I felt it was something that I was going to have to live with. I got tired of feeling tired and started to look into alternative medicine. I went on a program and can't believe how I feel now. I just got back from a six day backpacking trip in the Shenandoah National Park with my 20 year old daughter and kept up with her really well. I even did a 12 mile day and felt good afterwards."

In December '94 section hiker, trail maintainer, and active winter sports enthusiast, Donna Savluk, Ward's Girl, became pregnant with her first and only child. Along with her husband she carefully checked with her midwife about continuing her snowshoeing, skiing, and mountaineering activities through the winter. She climbed 14 White Mountain 4000-foot peaks over that winter and decided to get in some long distance hiking on the AT. Donna stood on Springer Mountain with a due date five months away. She hiked 164 miles to Fontana Dam and later attended the annual Trail Days celebration in Damascus where the ultrasound photo of her fetus won "Honorable Mention" in the hiker photo contest. "I went backpacking two weeks before my son was born. I hiked three days after my due date and later that day my water broke. I delivered my son after a 40-minute labor. Ethan is named after Ethan Crawford who cut the Crawford Path up Mt. Washington, the oldest continuously maintained footpath in the U.S. His initials are E.M.S. and while this doesn't entitle us to a discount at the store, at least everything is monogrammed for him!" Needless to say, Donna is an exceptional outdoorswoman with 15 years of rigorous and extensive backpacking experience in the strenuous White Mountains. For the vast majority of pregnant women, we are suggesting to just keep walking and get full approval of your doctor before hitting any trail.

Susan Roquemore, Dragon Lady, has been hypertensive since age 12 and medicated since her early 20's. "I found that in 1992 I was getting dizzy in the Smokies and cut back on meds and found that my blood pressure had dramatically dropped. I'd suggest periodic drug store checks along the way. I know my meds and am an RN well versed in adjusting medications so I wouldn't suggest this for everyone."

One woman epitomizes bravery and recovery. The first time she stepped foot on the AT was in 1993. The previous year she started rebuilding a life "that had previously been taken from me by my eating disorder," anorexia. She was 5'7" and weighed 100 pounds. Over the next few years she gained weight, backpacked different sections of the Trail, and became stronger and stronger. In '96, Melody Blaney, Midnite, thru-hiked the Appalachian Trail from Georgia to Maine.

Linda Bertoncini section hikes with her husband, Sonny, Mountain Lovers. "I went through a really tough period before I got into serious hiking…brain surgery and loss of all our material possessions when our house burnt down killing our three beloved pets, all in less than a year. After surgery 18 months ago I was unable to speak at all or walk unassisted. My doctors told my husband that I might not get any better than that."

My wonderful husband pushed me out on the Trail. At first, I hated it. My balance was so bad and each step was so difficult and painful. I fell and tripped constantly. As I got each single and long mile under my belt, I pushed myself just a little more. I will never forget my first 15 mile day without a pack in the Smokies. I was so proud of myself. That pride, and the confidence that the Trail empowered me with, gave me the incentive to push even harder. When I did that first 100 mile section hike, I was elated. I had a bad knee, lots of scratches and bruises from falling, but not a bruised spirit.

My balance is still poor, but with the Leki's now, I don't fall as much. And when I do, I just get up and feel grateful that I can walk. Sometimes I get mad and cry, but I get over it. When we did a section hike this past October, everything that could go wrong went wrong. Five hundred feet into the trail, on the very first day, I fell flat on my face. I hiked in constant pain, covered with bruises and a bump on my head.

If it weren't for hiking and the AT, I would probably be just like the other people I met in a head injury support group, loaded up on pain meds and antidepressants, complaining bitterly about their lives, talking about what they can't do. Hiking the AT has been a gift, a light that surrounds me even in the darkest day. The Trail has lifted me up and pushed me to continue living my life. I was very depressed but hiking the AT helped me put things into perspective. I began to see rainbows instead of storms. I experienced freedom and appreciation. It is as if crisis and tragedy were wiped away. I learned to take just one step at a time, one mountain at a time. Instead of rushing through life, I truly stop and smell the roses...watch the birds and butterflies. My relationship with my husband has been elevated to a higher dimension. Now my medication is just sitting on top of Springer and Blood Mountain and watching the sun set.

The doctors and therapists told me so many things I couldn't and would never be able to do. Mostly because of the AT and my husband's support, I have proved them all wrong. I am driving, started my own business, getting back into the real world, carrying on somewhat intelligent conversations and, most of all...HIKING. I am getting stronger and before too long I will do a thru-hike. I have to wait at least two years seizure free and work on improving balance and knee pain. I am 51 with four kids and three granddaughters. I feel younger than I have for years, thanks to the Trail. I plan on living and being healthy for many, many long years and proving wrong all my doctors and the people who have told me all the things I couldn't do. I can't wait to send them all postcards! I can, and I will.

Emergencies
Injuries-Illness-Home

Although the Appalachian Trail is considered a "footpath for those who seek fellowship with the wilderness," the reality, in most cases, is that you are never far from a road. None of our injured respondents have lamented about languishing for days before help arrived. Rescue operations can, however, become quite complex and demand the cooperation of fellow hikers and medical personnel. Hikers are strongly encouraged to be as self-sufficient as possible and prepared for all weather conditions with proper rain and cold weather gear, water, and food. One should never enter the woods unprepared and expect someone to help save them and foot the bill because they have been lax in their own planning and preparation. Loved

91

ones can be reassured that if an emergency arises on the home front, you can be reached often in a matter of hours.

Two time thru-hiker, Ginny Owen, Spirit Walker, describes the effectiveness of the Trail grapevine. "I have seen a few searches go out, and as long as people back home have a general idea of where you are, it doesn't take all that long to get an emergency message to a thru-hiker on the Trail. With the help of trail runners, maintainers, Forest Service personnel, e-mail list members, and the hikers themselves, a person can be found. It helps to sign in the registers, of course, especially if your family isn't following your trip closely. The Trail often runs near roads, and there are lots of side trails where the AT doesn't directly cross a road. Getting out wouldn't be difficult most of the time. One exception might be in the 100-mile wilderness in Maine when it could take two days to reach a road. Harder would be finding an airport to get you home."

One hiker suggested that the folks at home have a list of all the post offices along the Trail so that an emergency message can be relayed from the postmaster to a group of hikers. They in turn could post a message at a trail crossing in the vicinity of where the hiker might be. Signing both your real name and Trailname in the registers is recommended if you think your family might need to contact you. Younger hikers still living at home are especially encouraged to explain to parents that they may be out of touch for several days because the Trail does not conveniently pass a phone.

Section hiker, Jan Kerns, Tagalong, broke her leg when she was alone. She didn't panic, but prayed and kept her wits about her. Fortunately, within an hour, several hikers came by including her partner, Fran Godbey, Free Spirit, who was thought to be a day behind. With the help of many hikers, Jan was evacuated and taken to the hospital.

Joyce Scott, Poor Nameless Hiker, thru-hiked in '89 and broke her arm across the wrist while hiking in Pennsylvania. "I wrapped it in an ACE bandage and held it in a bandanna in my teeth." She then hiked to a shelter and spent, ironically, one of her few nights totally alone. "I left a note in the shelter, hiked three miles to the next road, hitched to the nearest town, and found a doctor who sent me to the nearest hospital via ambulance. I got a cast and advice specifically for hiking with a cast then hitched back to the

Trail for the night. All the medics who helped me for the next six weeks agreed to delay billing for six months and then to accept incremental payments. Be up front immediately on what you're doing." Joyce wore the cast to New Hampshire and notes that she learned to stuff her sleeping bag with her head and light her stove with her feet. No problem!

A mid-west hiker stresses getting to town immediately. "Don't be afraid to ask others, hikers and non-hikers for help. In one instance, the woman I'd been hiking with for a month fell and broke her arm. By asking others for help, we learned that the nearest road was two miles, not the 8 miles listed in the Data Book, and got a group of local bird watchers with a cell phone to call for an ambulance. Unfortunately, when I got giardia several months later, I failed to ask for help and spent many miserable days before other hikers arranged to have me taken off the Trail by someone vacationing in the area."

Jean Deeds, Indiana Jean, author of There are Mountains to Climb, broke her leg in Maine, the last state for a northbounder, after over 1,850 miles while hiking a stretch with her grown son. Greg was lucky to find a work crew of Harvard students supervised by an AMC (Appalachian Mountain Club) member, and Jean was evacuated out the next day. She recovered, wrote her book, started her speaking business, Stretch Your Limits, and returned to finish the Trail the following year adding the last chapter after summiting Katahdin.

Barbara DiGiovanni, D-Boss, relates her story. "My sister and I were hiking different sections of the Trail in north Virginia. I went to my cousin's in Lynchburg to visit when I finished my section while she finished the section she had missed. While there my brother called to say my Mom had died. I had cared for her for many years and this was most upsetting."

"How to find my sister? Easy. We always leave an approximate hiking plan with each other before we go so I hiked into the last shelter she could have reached by that date and looked to see if she had signed in. She hadn't so I left a note for her to hike to a specific location where I would be waiting. I went to the next shelter further south and noted that she had signed in. That narrowed the field. I also met a ranger who said she would put the word out that my sister was needed urgently. Meanwhile I drove to the gap and by a great coincidence she was having lunch there with some hiking buddies. This took about three hours. By 8 p.m. we were back in New York taking care of very sad business." Barbara also suggests that you contact home frequently and advise them of any change in your schedule. This way you won't feel obligated to cover the mileage you said you would if you don't want to.

Verna Soule, Gran'ma Soule, solo hiking on a seldom used trail, walked three days without seeing anyone. She fractured a bone in her foot and couldn't walk so set up her tent hoping it would be better in the morning. It wasn't. It was worse. She packed up, crawling on her hands and knees, then crawled a mile to a road dragging her backpack behind her. She got a ride to a doctor, then to a motel, and called her husband to come after her.

Stone heel and plantar fascitis were problems for Ellen Gibson, Steadfast Buffalo, on her section hike. The solution was better insoles and rest.

"When I started on the approach trail, I got blisters during the first hour of my hike," relates Nancy Marth, Geo, '97 thru-hiker. "They got worse the next day and for three days I had to hike in my Birkenstocks until I reached Neels' Gap. I took a week and a half off in order to heal my blisters and wanted to make sure that I wasn't getting back on the AT prematurely. There was never any question if I would get back on. It was just a matter of when. So don't get discouraged because some type of sickness or injury is common during a thru-hike."

A '98 hiker had to leave the Trail because of a foot injury occurring a mile from town. Even though she rested for a few days in town and returned to the Trail, her foot started hurting again and she knew a doctor's visit was in order. Even though she had to curtail her thru-hike, it did miracles for her anxiety disorder and she never had any problems on the Trail or since. "I think life being so simplified is what helped me a lot. Any stress I did have I had all day to think through and exercise out of me. My hike was very helpful. My faith in God, positive attitude, strength of spirit and determination are what actually got me through. All the other things I knew about hiking previous to my trip I would have figured out, by default, in the first few weeks."

Joyce Johnson, Pilgrim's Progress, has a story of perseverance. "I had my share of falls, and sometimes I was injured. I also had some severe bouts with diarrhea. At these times I usually didn't hike too many miles that day and took time to rest and recuperate. As a result of one bad fall after hiking 1,800 miles, I tore some tendons and cartilage in my left leg and knee. I had to stop and come home, Dr.'s orders, and then had a year of therapy."

"I returned two years later with my son. We hiked for over a hundred miles, and he became very sick with strep throat, flu, and a high temperature. We spent three or four days at a bed and breakfast off the Trail. The day we returned to the Trail, it rained 3 inches in less than one hour near Andover, Maine. The temperature dropped to 35 degrees and we almost froze. I even broke a tooth off from chattering my teeth, and my son got sick again. I had to quit. He had pneumonia and I could not risk his life; he was only twelve at the time. I will try for the third time to finish 160 miles in '99, my 10th year anniversary of when I first attempted to thru-hike. I will be 56 years old. But I'll do it!" Joyce started her thru-hike in '89 with the Trailname, Pilgrims Progress. In '92 she changed it to Pilgrim + one. When she returns to complete the Trail she will be Pilgrim-again!

Kathy Kelly Borowski sprained an ankle and had to walk 50 miles to town on it. She had the hiker flu (diarrhea and stomach upset), took the day off, and was fine the next day. "When I started the AT in March '88, my goal was to get halfway. Somewhere south of Damascus, my goal was to hike the whole thing. Due to an injury, I made it halfway. I then changed my goal to completing the Trail. I thought positive and made it. I just wanted to accomplish something on my own. I've proved there is a great deal I can do on my own. I did get help from time to time, but my desire kept me going."

Edna Williams writes, "I was very lucky. On each of the three times I broke my leg, I received help. Twice other hikers helped me by staying with me or going for help. The third time I was near a forest road and passers by on the road helped. Most of all, my guardian angel brought me the help!"

"More than being alone, I would worry more about lightning and hypothermia," all too familiar to Kelly Winters, Amazin' Grace. "On the Trail, other hikers will know where you are and where you're expected, and if you don't show up, they will often come looking for you. The second time I got hypothermia was up on Kinsman Mountain in New Hampshire on a dark, rainy, windy night. My flashlight blew out, and I was struggling along, desperate to get down, shivering and fairly incoherent. Other hikers had passed me that day and eventually realized something must be wrong. They came back looking with lights, and I'll always be grateful. They saved my life and guided me to warmth and shelter."

Kelly adds, "I got the flu twice, and both times holed up and rested until I could hike again. I twisted or sprained my ankle several times, wrapped it, and kept walking. You have to put up with a certain amount of pain on the Trail all the time and I think it makes you tougher; you keep going under adversities that would stop a normal person. If the sickness or injury is bad enough, rest is the best treatment. If it's really bad, you may have to leave the Trail. It takes a lot of mental toughness to put up with this stuff, but if you really want to thru-hike, you'll find it within yourself."

Susan Roquemeore, Dragon Lady, broke her leg on the AT and said it was a real pain! "What I did for a mile or so, was to 'hole up' and assess the damage. It helps that I am a nurse and can describe the injury in medical jargon. People came by and offered all sorts of help, but I waited two days before I knew I couldn't walk, then accepted help. Mainly, one needs to keep a clear head and take some time to make up your mind what to do about the situation. No panic about the entire thing, but I worried a bit about the rescue squad climbing that mountain to haul me out."

Lyme disease took Gail Johnson, Gutsy, by surprise in New England. "While I was thru-hiking I contracted Lyme disease. In Vermont I noticed I was feeling more tired than usual at the end of the day. I stopped bathing in the evenings. It was all I could do just to get to the shelter and get my water and eat supper. I attributed my exhaustion to the increased elevation gains in Vermont and not enough to eat. At Manchester Center I resupplied and went on. At the next shelter I stopped to rest. I was feeling lousy. I ached all over. I decided to hike out because I didn't want to be sick in a shelter. A day hiker came by and I told him I wasn't feeling well. I'm embarrassed to say I cried. He hiked down with me to the caretaker by the lake. I had the typical bulls-eye rash on my leg, but being from the south I'd never even heard of Lyme disease."

Gutsy went to several hospitals and eventually received an official diagnosis of acute Lyme disease. She started on antibiotics and the swelling on her foot lessened so she could get a shoe on and continue her hike. "At one shelter I met a doctor who was hiking the Trail. He told me that hiking was better than lying in bed. The exercise was helping the antibiotics work. For the rest of the hike my energy level was not what it had been. But little by little my energy did return and I finished the AT."

Cindy Miller, Mrs. Gorp, started the AT in '77 with intentions of completing that year. "By the time I reached Vermont, my deeply blistered heels and extreme homesickness contributed to my leaving the Trail. I did return in '79 and picked up where I left the Trail at the base of Bromley and completed the Trail for my honeymoon with my first husband." In '97 she hiked the Long Trail in Vermont and is also section hiking the Pacific Crest Trail.

A '97 hiker, Hilary Lang, Weatherwoman, describes herself as a big-chunk hiker. "I began what I thought would be a thru-hike in March '97. As it turns out, I would not have had enough money to finish the hike as I spent far more than I thought I would. I only made it to about halfway up the hill out of Bly Gap, North Carolina before I realized my knee was shot. I had to turn around and head back down to Hiawassee via a small dirt road not too far back. I used a couple of sticks and a very tightly wound ace bandage to splint it, and I essentially used my trekking poles as crutches to get the 3 miles out to the road. I had discovered I had torn up some more cartilage in my left knee after suffering from a skiing accident in '95."

Hilary spent the rest of the spring and summer hiking every weekend and building up the knee, lightening her pack, and then thru-hiked the Long Trail in Vermont in September where she was completely alone most of the whole hike. Her training included 350 AT miles in five different states-a big chunk, indeed. She returned to Springer in '98, did not repeat the approach trail from Amicolola Falls, and planned to be out a shorter period. Even though she had to leave the Trail due to a family crisis at home, she surprised herself. "I was out two months, did 500 miles, and thoroughly enjoyed every minute of it. The weather didn't bother me too much on this hike. We had some nasty stuff, too: tornadoes, hailstorms, several monsoons, two solid weeks of rain, and 10 inches of snow in the Smokies. I wasn't ready to leave when I had to go."

Pat Hatton, one half of The Mad Hatters, section hikes with her husband. She injured the plantar fascia on the bottom of her right foot as a result, she believes, of the stress involved in carrying too much weight for her size. "I feel it is important to emphasize carrying the proper packweight. I was unaware of the possible consequences of carrying too much weight and this is underemphasized in the literature." Hopefully, this book will provide some needed resources to help women hikers prevent unnecessary injuries.

Dealing with the Elements

Most hikers once they have experienced even a week of the Trail, would suggest that the weather, rather than any other factor, is the cause for most concern, anxiety, and safety considerations. Thunder and lightning storms, severe cold or blazing heat, and driving wet rain are a few of the conditions that can pose a real danger to the unprepared or naive hiker. Even though weather conditions pose the same concern to men and women, it is such a serious subject that it must be at least briefly mentioned within the context of this book. Future AT hikers are strongly encouraged to explore this subject further.

Christine Shaw, Firefly, details a potentially hazardous situation that can be a threat for hikers. "From my thru-hike in '96 I learned you must be prepared for not only the average weather, but also for the extremes. I was not prepared for the extremes, and I believe this nearly cost me my life on more than one occasion."

"Although Georgia is in the south, it can get darn cold down there. I had a stretch of three nights where the temperature was between -5 and

-15 degrees without the wind chill, and it never reached a high of even 20 during the whole week! That kind of cold is unusual and dangerous if you aren't ready for it. Several people became very sick. I had never before questioned whether or not I would survive the night. It puts a lot of things into perspective. A few weeks later we had a blizzard in the Smokies. Snow drifts were over 10 feet deep. Snowshoes would have been a great help. Nearly everyone got severely sunburned from the glare, and most people ran low on food at some point because in those kinds of conditions you can only go 5-10 miles per day. Then one day it sleeted, I got wet, and four of us got mildly hypothermic. This was still in the deep snow, so going to town from the middle of the Smokies was not an option. I also got frostbite on my toes, not a pleasant experience and something I would definitely recommend trying to avoid."

Christine recommends listening to the weather forecasts and assume the worst. "It is better to be prepared for the storm and be pleasantly surprised by a nice day than vice-versa. That seems like common sense, but it is amazing how many hikers, including myself, ignore this and find themselves in trouble. You can never underestimate the awesome power of Mother Nature. The minute you do, she will teach you a lesson you will never forget."

Jeanne Spellman suggests watching the weather and found hypothermia to be the real danger on the Trail. "I carried a couple of instant soups that I could cook quickly in a hypothermia emergency. Watch for signs of hypothermia in other hikers you see. Try not to go over a summit when a thunderstorm is imminent. Plan lunches and breaks around getting over a bare summit before the storm. Check the trees above your tent for dead branches before pitching your tent if a storm or high winds are threatening."

Joyce Johnson, Pilgrim's Progress, was close to Clingman's Dome in a lightning storm. "I actually felt the hair raise on the back of my neck and arms. I threw off my external frame pack as fast as I could, knelt down on my sleeping pad, waited and prayed for the storm to pass. A girl a few miles behind me was struck the same day and was injured, but survived."

Carol Donaldson, Coosa, suggests learning to read the sky and clouds and be prepared with appropriate clothing, gear, and supplies. "The elements of the AT are wind, rain, snow, and sun with the threat of dehydration. Hikers must drink more than the usual amounts of water, no matter what the season of the year. Sometimes, women tend to drink less because they don't have the easy accessibility to urinating as men do. By the time a woman starts feeling thirsty, not a reliable measure of actual body thirst, she is already a quart low and this can greatly effect hiking performance."

"Never trust the weather on the AT." Sarah Dixon saw snow, sleeting rain, hair-raising lightning, trails lost in fog, and sweltering heat. "The most important thing in my experience is having enough extra socks so when you tramp through the rain all day you have dry socks for the next day. What is more important than healthy feet? Gaitors help, too. I had a poncho that I found to be just perfect for the rain. Rain suits just don't breathe enough so you're just as wet on the inside as on the out!"

How to Pee with your Pack On!

Women hikers will agree that one of the most highly prized outdoor skills is learning to pee with your pack on...in a rainstorm! Find a woman who can perform this feat, and you will have found an experienced backpacker. While men can stand and deliver, women often need to take a more creative approach, preferably one that won't make them have to take off a too heavy pack which means inevitably having to hoist it on again. Some women can pee while standing by moving aside their shorts with liners. This does take practice, however. Zanika makes a line of clothing with pull aside fabric so you can pee without dropping your drawers. Other hikers just stand straight upright with legs spread wide. Washing hands before and/or after urination may be unrealistic and some women choose to shake and use a panty liner. As already mentioned, it is imperative to remain hydrated while hiking. The skill of peeing quickly, accurately, and frequently is one of real value.

One hiker suggests that when squatting becomes a challenge with blown muscles and you can't stand, find a nice fallen log, lean your butt against it, and leave plenty of room to pee. A log with a view is preferred.

100

When you pee in a privy, leave your toilet paper there. On the Trail, keep a separate Ziploc for storing used T.P. It is not necessary to carry out toilet paper after a bowel movement. The current soil conditions of the Trail allow for adequate degrading of solid waste.

Women have creative solutions for peeing at night without leaving the warmth and comfort of their tents. One carries an empty peanut butter jar; another a large freezer Ziploc bag that is emptied in the woods in the morning, rinsed, and stashed in a side mesh pocket of her pack. When you pee in your tent, make sure you move your sleeping bag and pad aside first in case you miss. If you have a vestibule, place the Ziploc outside, securely closed. Learning this handy skill keeps you from having to wander around outside at night.

"Privacy in the early spring before the leaves fill out the tree branches is tricky, but I found that the guys on the Trail were always respectful. They got pretty casual themselves though, if they got to know you, and I guess, thought of you as just one of the guys. I did comment to one friend I was hiking with, 'Gosh, darn, you could step off the Trail at least five feet!' I was a little envious of the guys. They could just relieve themselves without taking their packs off. Some of us gals worked pretty hard at figuring out a technique to do this ourselves. I gave up when I tried, in pouring rain, to get my Lycra tights back up, with my pack still on. I hope no one witnessed that dance."

"I find that irrigation and fertilization moments are best handled with the least fuss. I know some women who feel they have to hike completely out of view of the Trail, and the effort ends up drawing attention to the fact they are voiding themselves. Sometimes this is neither safe nor practical, especially in steep terrain. To pee, I try to find the shelter of an off-trail tree or rock. Watch out for snakes and do it quickly. For more major business, I think it's most sanitary, from the standpoint of spreading diseases, to go further off trail, preferring downhill and FAR from water sources. I generally avoid using TP, but I am pretty nuts about washing up after a BM." Many women pack a trowel or use their boot heel and a stick for digging a cat hole at least 6-8 inches deep and cover it over after making a BM. If you do decide to use soft leaves and moss, make sure you can identify them.

A section hiker regretted not doing her Kegels (exercises designed to tighten the muscles around the vagina and rectum) before starting her section hike. "I don't know if it was the constant walking or whether I just waited too long to stop, but I almost couldn't 'hold it' long enough to get the pack off and pants down. I finally disciplined myself to stop as soon as I felt the need to go and it was a little better." Another woman suggests that just before putting on that pack in the morning and after every break, be conscious of the need to urinate and go even if you think you might not need to. Then you won't feel that you are constantly interrupting your hike."

Partners can always serve as lookouts for breaks in the woods. Susan Roquemore tries to see the humorous side to every situation. "My husband knows I pee on the average of about every fifteen minutes while old 'camelbladder' can wait until there's a tiled urinal installed on the AT in a Trail shelter."

Dealing with your Period on the Trail

Like learning to take care of bathroom needs in the Trail environment, a woman having her period needs to find what works for her while following low impact environmentally conscious techniques. It is not acceptable to bury used sanitary products no matter how deep! Although some women suggest burning in a very hot fire, the acceptable method is to pack ALL used products out. You can throw toilet paper in privies but DO NOT throw used sanitary products. Be considerate. Think of the volunteer Trail maintainer who has to deal with your laziness. Wrapping them in tin foil and putting them in a Ziploc bag with some pre-crushed aspirin already in the bag or, as one woman suggested...pine needles, will reduce the odor.

In a shelter, keep sanitary supplies with you, in or near your sleeping bag, so you can change right in your bag in the morning before you get up. This prevents any awkwardness and embarrassment you may feel struggling to get to your backpack. Remember, just as you hang your food and toiletries and don't cook or eat in your tent, you must also hang your used sanitary products. Use a double Ziploc so as not to attract critters.

It is very common for a woman to experience changes in her menstrual cycle. It helps to be aware that these changes are normal considering the stress and vigorous nature of the thru-hiking experience. Some women find that birth control pills keep them regular so they at least know when to expect their period. Women were very open and honest describing their personal experiences in handling their periods in the woods environment.

"When I was a young woman," writes Amazon Queen, "It never seemed to fail. I would strap on a pack, take ten steps on the Trail, and my period would start whether it was time or not. And, of course, it would be the heaviest in female history. Ever since then, I have carried a week's supply of tampons, pads, and ibuprofen, if not for me, then to share with anyone else in need. One time two friends were out with a group of 10 girls and almost every single one of them started, and no one had any supplies. I find that cramping is less on the Trail because, for some reason the weight of the pack relieves it."

"I was 43 during my thru-hike and still menstrual. My periods were delayed and much lighter than usual. My usual cramps and bloating were significantly less. This made the management of my period much simpler during the hike."

"My periods (I take estrogen and progestin and still have periods) were much shorter when I was hiking, maybe 2 1/2 days. I absolutely hate using tampons but after the first time on the AT, I realized that you can't wear pads and walk 12 miles without some serious chafing. So I used Playtex tampons with a plastic applicator. Save the applicators and used tampons in a trash Ziploc and dispose of them properly when you get to town! I can't tell you how disgusting it is to see those items on the ground in a toilet area near a shelter. It reflects on all women whether we've been guilty or not. I also used a mini-pad just in case. Remember, you probably aren't going to change underwear daily. If you do, your pack is too heavy and you're spending too much time and energy washing and drying clothes when you get to camp. Plus you're too obsessed."

"I found that my periods were more regular and less heavy while

103

hiking. One thing to remember is to always carry out sanitary products like tampons. You should never bury your toilet paper or waste products because animals dig them up and litter them all over the Trail. It can get pretty bad with all of the overcrowding. I also suffer from really bad cramps. I just had to make sure to bring lots of ibuprofen. If I had cramps too bad, I took a day off, either in the shelter or in the town. Exercise is very good for the system, making it less painful for periods."

"I put tampons and panty liners in my mail drops. I bought the tampons in a cellophane wrapper, without the applicator, so I generated less waste. Since my periods were much lighter, the tampons and panty liners were all I needed. I used the panty liners during cold weather even when I didn't have my period, and shook rather than used toilet paper each time I peed. I changed the liners every two or three days and was able to keep my shorts relatively clean. Used liners were put in a Ziploc lock bag with other trash and deposited at trashcans as we passed them along the Trail. During warm weather I found I sweated too much for the liners to be useful, but was able to wash my shorts often with stream water and put them back on to dry." Some women wear dark shorts during their period.

"I had a real problem with my periods while hiking. I was 46 and on the verge of menopause. I flowed so heavily some days and nights I almost hemorrhaged twice. I carried heavy, hospital type pads and would leak through two of these onto my clothes and sleeping bag at night. I had to get up at dawn and find a private place and take care of cleaning up. The harder I hiked, the worse it was so I had to stop hiking and stay off the Trail and rest for one or two days until the situation was better. Of course, disposing of the pads was also a problem with so many used. I just wrapped them and put them in plastic bags until I could find a trashcan. As I did with ALL my trash, I carried it out."

"My periods stopped by the third cycle. Though I lost 10 pounds during the first half of the AT, I must have lost enough body fat to effect that wonderful change. Periods did resume after being home for two months."

A woman's body can also react differently at varying times in her life. "On my first thru-hike, my period stopped entirely for the entire time

I was hiking. I wasn't as lucky the second time, but I noticed that my period was a lot lighter. Another factor for some thin women is that when body fat gets below a certain percentage, the periods will stop, which is exactly what can happen on a thru-hike."

Although not a serious trend in hiking circles at this time, some women have resorted to getting a shot, depo-provera, to stop their periods for three months at a time. Not every one has the same results with the shot and you can end up spotting unpredictably.

Nothing seems to excite women quite so much as a discussion about The Keeper, a one ounce diaphragm like reusable soft rubber menstrual cup that can be inserted manually to catch menstrual flow. The cup itself is about 2 inches long with a small extension of rubber that serves like a tampon string. It is shorter and thicker and can be trimmed to fit you.

One woman described it as looking barbaric, fairly thick and stiff like a plumbing device, and the color of a UPS truck. Insertion can sometimes be a problem or impossible due to one's personal anatomical structure. Women have reported that it takes a few sometimes awkward uncomfortable trials to get the hang of it. The Keeper has a life expectancy of ten years. Women considering using one on a thru-hike should practice a few months before their hike to make sure the fit is right for their body. Women on the list who have used The Keeper recommend emptying it out several times a day, especially before bedtime. Wash hands before and after with filtered water if possible and clean the keeper. You can leave one in for even up to 12 hours. When hiking, the contents are buried in a cathole and covered over. Just don't drop it into the privy if you are at a shelter area!

A number of women expressed concern about the incidence of yeast infections while thru-hiking and list members had a number of suggestions for keeping this under control. Stress, diet, and the sweaty conditions of hiking may produce ideal conditions for yeast growth. The use of the pill and/or antibiotics will increase the likelihood of infection. Antibiotics kill the good bacteria and allow the yeast to grow.

One hiker, when feeling on the verge of an infection, would walk without underwear. She wore a full elastic waist cotton skirt that fell above

105

the knee. Running shorts, often purchased in the men's department, with integral liners also provide good ventilation.

Several women recommended acidolpholus tabs. They can also be combined with warm water and directly applied, if you're already terribly uncomfortable. Yogurt can be dehydrated into a leather of sorts and packed away for munching and as a preventative measure. A nurse on the list recommends Difulcan tablets for a one pill treatment. Having a tent for taking care of hygienic needs can provide needed privacy for women hikers.

Is PMS a Factor during a Thru-Hike?

"I have to smile," writes Dania Egedi, Lightweight. "I had been having an ongoing argument with my significant other before the Trail as to whether my mood changed around my period. I was convinced it was him. Spending time by myself with no one else around made me realize just how my moods changed around my period. Now that I am more aware of it, it is easier for me to handle off the Trail. Certainly the consequences of PMS on the Trail were less. No matter how much you yell at your pack or that stupid log you just tripped over, you don't have to apologize later."

Melissa Sumpter, Selky, writes from the Trail that the most important aspect of this whole experience has been getting to know herself not only mentally but also physically. "Watching your body as it changes from stored fat to toned muscle, knowing your body's limits and feeling its pain. Being aware of your cycle and how exercise decreases the pain and flow to nearly nothing. I rejoice in having the time to notice the cyclical changes my body goes through month to month. You're aware of your moods and how they change your mind frame. You have time to think about those feelings and deal with them instead of pushing them aside and masking them with the motions of everyday life. You have the time and space to acknowledge your changes and deal with them. That's important to me."

"PMS is something I'm experiencing at the moment. I have found myself much more emotional out here on the Trail. Some days I feel like crying for no good reason at all. The slightest thing can sometimes send me to the brink of tears. I think that all the time I have to myself to think makes the emotions so much more recognizable."

"Yep, you're gonna get it," adds Kelly Winters, Amazin' Grace. "Someday when you're sweating up some mountain and cursing it and fate in general, or having fits of random anger and unscheduled crying, you'll realize, 'Hey, I've got PMS. That's what my problem is'."

Larissa Smith said she did not notice the usual symptoms she got at home. "I did feel much more tired and had less energy when my period started but my flow was less than usual."

Kay Cutshall, The Old Gray Goose, says she must be one of those old gals who are fortunate not to have horrendous mood swings and was not really bothered by 'hot flashes' while on the Trail. "If anything they were LESS then than now. Do these things ever end? Menses have paused and I was just glad I didn't have to worry about them while I was hiking."

Hilary Lang, Weatherwoman, writes about PMS on her '98 section hike. "I definitely PMSed on the Trail, and most of the women I've talked to say it's worse out there than at home. It was worse for me, as well. I don't really know why, except that maybe your emotions tend to run much closer to the surface out there; it's harder to bury them. I had one horrible day this year that involved a PMS-induced temper tantrum, which lasted for 20 minutes...because my tarp fell off my pack, of all things. After I calmed down, realizing how silly it had been, I decided to stay put a bit. I just dropped my pack and sat on it for almost another hour, even though I had only hiked a mile, and listened to the birds and the wind and soaked up the sun. I guess I just hadn't paid attention before to what was going on around me and to what I really needed...which was some peace and quiet."

Privacy
Changing + Basic Cleanliness/ The Little Extras

Women hikers adopt a no fuss, no muss attitude while on the Trail itself. At home they may have make-up cases that weigh as much as their packs on the Trail. While hiking their toiletries kit usually fits into a small Ziploc bag. Being filthy, dirty, and smelly are the realities of the hiking experience and everybody is in the same situation.

What every woman decides to do at the end of her hiking day varies very little. On the Trail, most follow a minimal wash-up routine often with cold water and sometimes with a heated cup of water and a few drops of biodegradable soap. In town or whenever the opportunity lends itself, well, that's another story. The razors, usually sent to maildrops, may or may not come out, and it's definitely a call for long hot showers, deep soaking tubs, and a stop for a massage and immersion in a hot tub going through Hot Springs. Some make a trip to a salon for a haircut although as Jo-Ellen Kimmel, Mummyfoot, reported, "The beautician insisted on washing my hair three times before she would do anything with it." Whatever the Trail washing routine, one needs to follow low impact techniques. All washing should be done away from the water source other hikers are using for drinking and cooking water.

"I love being a scrub!" Amanda Henck a recent high school graduate, list member, and future thru-hiker enthusiastically wrote. "The Trail is my excuse to be a scrub. I put my hair in pigtail braids and cover them with a hat and do minimal stuff to keep all that clean." Although Amanda revels in dirt, she says she always puts on clean clothes and wipes down 'a bit' to keep her sleeping bag clean. Like Amanda, women with long hair keep it up under a hat or bandanna but some also opt for really short haircuts, a sort of modified buzz. Women going gray who usually color their hair...well, they just let nature take its course.

"I am not really bothered by a bit of dirt," reports another young woman. "I used wet wipes to keep my hands and face clean and that was good enough for me. I found I always got dirtier if it was raining; I somehow always ended up covered in mud. I never shaved and didn't carry

108

a comb. The only time I washed my hair or showered was when I was in town. I brushed my teeth and flossed every day." Many women use baby wipes or wet wipes but some consider that a luxury item adding extra pack weight. Taking deodorant is also considered unnecessary pack weight, but the occasional woman did report that she felt better having the travel variety along.

Kelly Winters, Amazin' Grace, says she never met a hiker who cared about basic good grooming. "If having certain things clean feels good to you and you are able to keep them clean, then do it. My teeth and my underwear were the only parts of me that were as clean as they are in civilization. You will have to give up a lot of your civilized ideas about needing to wear clean clothes, have clean hair, and shower every day. On the Trail, it's just not possible. You're going to stink, have black fingernails, and hair so greasy it's waterproof, at least some of the time. If you're the kind of person who is overly obsessed with all the things women 'should' or 'are supposed to' do to their bodies to please other people, do yourself a favor and take a vacation from it."

Kelly was fortunate as a girl. "My family was very outdoorsy. I was lucky and belonged to a Girl Scout troop that did real, get-dirty-and-sweat camping and hiking. More girls need this! If you are in a position to pass nature- knowledge to a girl, please do it."

"After two weeks of hiking on the AT, privacy is no longer an issue," says Carolyn Cunningham, Tawanda. "On the Trail, the outdoors, without walls, becomes home for everyone. If I felt awkward changing in front of other hikers, I'd wander off to the privy, change inside my sleeping bag, or set up my tent. With all the other necessities to worry about at the end of the day, such as cooking food and resting your feet, privacy becomes irrelevant."

"During my thru-hike," writes Rachel Dubois, Solophile, there were only a few times I felt the absolute need to wash my hair on the Trail. I would fill my 2-gallon water bag with unfiltered water, find a spot a hundred or so feet from the water source, hang the bag on a tree, and enjoy a wonderful hair washing with a little bit of Dr. Bonner's soap. I tried not to wet my hair in streams just because of the soap or hair gel residue that

I was worried about rinsing out of my hair." Some women take nail clippers, a small comb, nail file, or a folding wash basin.

Solophile felt at times an indescribable need to reclaim some little bit of femininity. "After months on the Trail, you can get to feeling quite androgynous. I combated this with a few little luxuries that really carried a long way. I took to wearing a pair of earrings! I had also packaged some little feminine pampering things in my maildrops: hair gel, conditioner, and a very pleasant smelling lotion in each drop box. I had packaged them up in single use sizes with my seal-a-meal. I looked forward to that lotion more than I can say. Just the thought of being able to smell good for a 12 hour period while in town was enough to get me through my stinky days."

"My other extravagance was carrying a 'scrubby glove' with me the entire length of the Trail. It's one of those bright pink gloves made of some sort of plasticy type material, weighs less than an ounce, dries almost instantly, retains no odors, and is absolutely great at scrubbing off dirt, grime, dead skin, and making you feel clean, soft, and refreshed again. Take every bit of enjoyment and pampering you can get while you're out there as long as it doesn't mean more than an ounce or two of extra weight."

Christine Shaw, Firefly, rejoices in dirt. "Maybe it's because I am pretty young, but gosh, I love to get dirty! My thru-hike was perfect for this. Seriously though, I actually found that the absolute most difficult part of not showering for a week or more was putting that same hiking shirt on every morning. I found that although my body was definitely producing it's own amazing aroma, my shirt was absolutely toxic. For me to stay sane out there, I did a few simple things. First of all, I would rinse my shirt every few days. This produced a world of difference. If any article of my clothing started standing up on its own, I would rinse it immediately. On particularly hot and drippy days I often rinsed off with a swim somewhere. I usually kept my long black hair back in a braid or bun, so although it looked really greasy all the time, it wasn't really a big concern cause it was never in my way. The best thing I did at the end of those long tough days was wash my face. You feel like a different person after that. It makes you feel human again, and maybe even a little like a woman!"

Amazon Queen has mastered the art of the quick change. "After years of struggling with dressing and undressing in my sleeping bag, I realized that the men in the shelter were really not interested in what I was doing. In fact, they were careful to avert their eyes. I developed some ways to make it easier on myself and still maintain modesty. While it is still light, I go out into the woods and take care of any clean up and change into whatever shirt I plan to wear to bed. During menstruation, I have my supply bag handy so that I can quickly grab it and slip away. When it is bedtime, I sit on my unzippered bag and remove my long pants, pull the covers up and zip up. Then I get in the bag, unhook my bra and pull it through my shirtsleeves. I reverse the process in the morning. What I have found is that the men have been conscious about protecting their privacy with women present."

Vicki McMahan suggests, "You can always step away from the shelter a little if you need some privacy. One of the easiest ways to handle your clean up times is to always wear a jog bra. You can just take off your top, wash up as you wish and pull on a clean shirt. If you need to change clothes completely, you can either ask for a few minutes of private time behind the shelter or just crawl into your sleeping bag and with a minimum of acrobatics just change inside the bag!"

"I found hikers to be very respectful of personal privacy," notes Sue Freeman, Blueberry. Men and women simply asked others to look away while they changed in a shelter. The request was granted without hesitation. If you really wanted privacy, you only had to walk into the woods behind some bushes, weather permitting. We had one situation where a guy arrived at a full shelter drenched to the skin on a cold rainy evening. We shoved over to let him sleep at the feet of other hikers and encouraged him to change into dry clothes. He was groggy and not acting right-on the verge of hypothermia. We helped him peel off his wet clothes and put dry ones on in the midst of everyone. Modesty was the least of our worries at that point. Basically, on the Trail people are more concerned with each other's safety than with sexuality."

Jan Kerns, Tagalong, learned the technique of changing clothes and sponge bathing with wet wipes in her mummy style sleeping bag. "It's a little difficult if you have very long legs to bend them up to slip clothing over the feet, but it can be done." Kay Cutshall, The Old Gray Goose, suggests a direct, "OK, turn your heads, gotta get changed."

"All you need is a roll of toilet paper, a toothbrush and a small tube of toothpaste and you could go for a month!" writes another woman. "BUT the luxury I have recently discovered that I cannot live without are...baby wipes." Other helpful items include contact lenses, case and lubricant, suncreen, tweezers for ticks and eyebrows, and a small mirror in case something gets stuck in your eye.

A section hiker says she never wears foundation or other make-up but on her 200-mile hike, her nod in the direction of civilization was a light pink lipstick put on with the aid of a small mirror. "I know, I know. We're talking extra ounces here. But, for me, it was important and no matter how cold or dripping wet or smelly I was, that little nod in the morning and before going into town made me feel better. P.S. I also justified the mirror as a signaling device, though thankfully never needed to use it for that."

Another section hiker adds, "The Trail is the Trail. Everybody wears the same four pieces of clothing. These are somewhat dirty and very certainly stinky. Privacy is not much of a problem. Everybody eats, drinks, sleeps, changes, and grooms pretty much in front of everybody else. We are all hairy and smell to high heaven. We all love this, or at least accept a certain degree of it between towns. Everybody is cool with it including me. Why then, do I need my eyeliner?" On sharing this most "aberrant" of hiking behaviors with the women's list, she was assured that although there are more important things to worry about i.e., lightning storms, hypothermia, staying hydrated and well nourished, she could do whatever she wanted to do. It's really none of anybody's business, and she should continue with her little "addiction" if that made her a happy hiking woman.

Finding privacy to take a quick wash, change clothes, or go to the bathroom, can be seen as real challenges if you are very modest. You can also choose to deal with these situations in a more matter of fact easygoing manner. Most shelter areas have a privy (outhouse) where a woman can change a tampon and you can change clothes in a privy, behind a shelter, or simply alert the guys to look the other way. Jeanne Spellman once had a male hiker thank her for being easy to share a shelter with and because she respected her own privacy. As a consequence, most men also did their washing and changing out of her sight.

Many women just prefer to carry a tent making their Trail lives a whole lot simpler. If you feel privacy will be an issue for you, just take a tent and trim pack weight with other items as most women do. Dot MacDonald, D-Trail, always carries a tent. "I may need privacy, couldn't make it to the shelter in time, may not want to join the townies in their Saturday night bash, feel like being alone, or the shelter leaked. I usually stay at shelters because of the camaraderie, the ease of cooking, and because I can see the night sky."

Are there Special Nutritional Needs
for Women Thru-hikers?

Registered dietician and '97 thru-hiker Sherri Swartz, Sunrise, explains that the biggest nutritional needs for both men and women are water and calories. Drink enough water so that you urinate at least every 4 hours during the day and make sure urine is clear or pale yellow. Sports drinks aren't really necessary because you'll be snacking enough to get plenty of sodium and electrolytes. You can add a flavored drink powder to plain water so you'll drink more and get some extra calories in the sugar.

Sherri warns against skimping on food on the Trail and gorging in town. "Do your best to eat enough to be satisfied, both on and off the Trail. This can be a dilemma for a woman having to carry extra food weight when hiking alone when she doesn't want to hitchhike to town very often." Sherri thru-hiked with her husband, seldom carried more than 4 days of food, and resupplied at very small towns or country grocery stores less than a mile from the Trail. That way they didn't even bother hitchhiking, and the stop didn't take a lot of time from their hike.

The main nutrient needs that are especially high for women are calcium and iron, Sherri adds. Calcium is important for women of all ages and iron is most important for pre-menopausal women. The best sources of calcium on the Trail are cheese and dried milk, which can be mixed into

113

puddings or cereals. Most kinds of nuts and dried beans also have a fair amount of calcium, and when eaten in large quantities can supply a good chunk of your needs. I would still recommend calcium supplements for all women hikers just to be sure. They're very safe and inexpensive. I took 1200 mg of calcium per day, in addition to instant pudding with dry milk once a day and gorp with mixed nuts.

Most grain foods such as cereals, breads, rice, and pasta are fortified with iron. With the amount of foods you will be eating per day, you will probably meet your needs. Still, a multivitamin with 100% RDA of iron, not more, might be a good idea especially if you tend to have heavy periods. Lack of iron can lead to anemia which can really cut down your energy level on the Trail.

As far as other vitamins and trace minerals are concerned, include some canned meat or dried beans and dried fruit and/or dried vegetables every day. It's really hard to get enough fruits and vegetables on the Trail so a basic multivitamin can help fill the gaps. Try to eat lots of fruits and veggies in town, too. Since almost all foods contain some protein, you'll get enough just because you're eating so much food. Be sure you're getting enough of the essential amino acids including legumes (nuts and beans), meat, or dairy products twice a day. Lentils and split peas are great for vegetarians because they're light and you don't have to soak them.

Fiber can often be an important nutrient on a thru-hike especially for older women. It's no fun to be constipated out in the woods in the rain or in a really rank privy! This can be a problem especially at the beginning of the hike. Eat plenty of dried fruit (prunes really are the best), and be sure you're drinking enough water. Nuts, beans, dried vegetables, and whole grain cereals and crackers can supply fiber, too. Once you get used to the Trail and to exercising more, you'll probably have less constipation than before you were on the Trail.

Sherri adds a final word about the best Trail food out there-gorp. It has more calories per ounce than anything except plain butter or peanut butter which you wouldn't eat alone anyway. The nuts supply lots of monounsaturated fat (the healthiest kind), protein, iron, calcium, fiber, and lots of trace vitamins and minerals. The dried fruit has concentrated sugar,

114

vitamins A and C, and fiber. The M+M's give you a chocolate fix! Unfortunately, it is also a food that many people pack too much of too early and then get sick of it so resort to eating less nutritional sugary snacks and candy bars instead.

I would recommend either making or buying several different kinds of gorp. Choose different kinds of nuts and fruits for each. Add special things to some mixes such as coconut and extra M+M's and put them each maildrop. Remember you will probably not have a 'trail appetite' your first couple of weeks so you don't have to start out with a huge bag of gorp or other foods. Most people I observed on the Trail brought too much food at the beginning and too little food for the rest of the hike.

Lisa Barter, Tinkerbell, is a vegetarian and thru-hiked in '97. She bought most of her food in bulk and aside from basic snacks like GORP, candy bars and nutritional bars, ate things like polenta, lentils, black beans and rice, couscous, falafel, veggie burger mix, dried soups, and dehydrated vegetables. Snacks, breakfasts, and lunches shouldn't pose a problem but Lisa suggests checking out a local health food store for economical bulk items for maildrops and dehydrating before the hike.

Many hikers have food cravings and when they get to town pile their plates high with salads, foods with calcium, and fruit. Craving potato chips? You probably need salt. Bananas? Potassium. That's what Dania Egedi, Lightweight, craved. "I am a vegetarian and got into a protein deficiency on the Trail. It caused me muscle problems coming into Hot Springs and was something I had to keep an eye on the rest of the Trail. You have to listen to your body."

Women &Thru-Hiking on the Appalachian Trail

Chapter three

AFTER

Motivation

When the going gets tough, how does a thru-hiker keep driving herself to reach her goal? What is it that compels those 10-15% of starters to push on state after state, month after month? The majority of thru-hikers leaving the Trail are not injured? Of the injured, how many could have prevented their injuries by doing fewer miles in an effort to avoid stress fractures, not hiking when exhausted and with energy resources depleted, and taking care of hot spots before they became infected blisters?

Dania Egedi, Lightweight, almost quit. "Aside from an injury early on when I was concerned that I wouldn't be able to do it physically, I came close to quitting in Pennsylvania. It was a drought year, and there was little or no water along the Trail. Kind people were leaving water jugs at Trail crossings for thru-hikers. There was never enough. We had to carry what water we could for long distances. I had never hiked in the summer before, and the salt from sweating and the contact with my pack rubbed my back raw. I also had salt blisters along my thighs, on the backs of my knees, and in the crook of my arm and groin."

"As I came into New York, I was ready to quit. I stayed the night at Greymoor Monastery and called a friend to come pick me up. He told me to sleep on my decision and call him in the morning. I had good food that night, lots of liquids, and the Monastery was very peaceful. I had some conversations with the monks, nothing earth shattering, but some combination of the food, water, and peacefulness made me decide to tough it out another day. And then another. And then another. The weather didn't break until I reached Connecticut. I got through it the same way I got up a difficult climb, one step at a time. I knew that I could get through another day of this misery but not a whole week. So I got through one day. And then the next, and pretty soon it had been a whole week. This has been my most enduring lesson from the Trail."

"It is the mental challenge to keep hiking that is difficult," emphasizes Nancy Marth, Geo. "My motivation to keep going was multi-faceted. Although sometimes I don't like being this way, I am goal-oriented. This meant that I wanted to finish no matter what. Some people might say, 'Well, if you weren't enjoying the trip anymore, why kill yourself to get to the end.' Yes, there were many times in the remaining weeks of my hike when I wanted to quit, but it only made me try harder and challenge myself to get past certain hurdles and enjoy those remaining weeks."

"So I mentally motivated myself to see as much beauty as I could in any situation and to laugh away the frustrations of hiking day after day in rain and mud. It worked for the most part, but there were those times when it didn't work. It was then I discovered my limits."

"Motivation also came from always wanting to see what was just ahead...around the corner...up the mountain...down near the stream. I wanted to experience every part of the Trail. Simply, motivation came from knowing myself, challenging myself, and knowing that I wouldn't feel satisfied if my trip weren't completed."

On the AT, hikers set daily goals. They always save a little bit of energy every evening for planning the next day's hike. Completing each state is a goal in itself. The miles add up and the months pass by. One does not reach Katahdin in a haphazard fashion. Being goal oriented goes hand in hand with planning and preparation and is a necessary aspect of successfully completing a thru-hike.

Christine Shaw, Firefly '96, was greatly supported by her hiking companions when the going got rough. "I was lucky enough to miss the

118

Virginia Blues, but something much worse hit me mid-New Hampshire, and lasted all the way to that last teary step on Katahdin. I believe it was a combination of stresses: exhaustion, malnutrition, and homesickness. Did I say exhaustion? It was really bad when I hit Gorham, and I almost went home on several occasions. At that point, I had already been out for six months, lost 60 pounds, and was ready to go back to school. It was a really hard time. My determination not to quit was fighting pretty hard with my dreams of family, friends, and stationary living. My Trail friends dragged me to the end. Halfway up Katahdin they even had to convince me to continue. That tells you how strong that force was."

"As hard as it got, I still loved being in the outdoors. I never lost that and I'm planning to thru-hike again in '99. I'm going to try for a shorter hike, though, because I believe the near seven month trip was what did me in. I also probably would have liked Maine better if I hadn't been hit by three hurricanes. Not ideal conditions...but we made it."

"I think in the end it depends on how much you want it. If you can't picture yourself standing on top of Katahdin, it will be really hard to get through those tough moments. But then I know some people who didn't picture it until they were there. I guess it is really personal, but I found picturing myself in victory helped me take that next step."

Visualization seems to be an important factor for many thru-hikers. Some even have a distinctly clear picture of how they want to see themselves at the end. It is usually standing atop the summit sign on Katahdin in triumph. Perhaps those who have that mental picture of themselves completing the Trail have an extra-added advantage. Certainly the Christmas cards and holiday greetings sent throughout the country with the hiker's photo atop Katahdin is an indication that the process of visualization has a critical value worth considering. Visualization is cost effective and doesn't add to your packweight.

What were your goals for hiking
the Appalachian Trail from end-to-end?

Regina Erskine, Whispering Pine, echoes the words of many goal oriented determined women. "It was imperative that I made it from end-to-end. I would have been very disappointed with myself if I hadn't completed my thru-hike. No matter how tough things got at times, it was never an option to get off the Trail. In some ways, unfortunately, this goal conflicted with my goal to relax and enjoy my journey." Another hiker said that only a death in the family or a broken leg would have made her end her hike.

"I don't know that I really had any expectations the first time I hiked," writes Sarah Dixon. "I came away with far more than I ever could have expected. The second time I wanted to finish and couldn't. I was very disappointed at being unable to achieve my goal. I had expected more from myself. I have changed my perspective of my old friend the AT though, and the next time my expectations will be different. Day by day."

Kay Cutshall, The Old Gray Goose, wanted to hike the Appalachian Trail end-to-end. "Actually, my goal was to hike in one continuous journey as a thru-hike, but I left the Trail before I did that. I decided I still wanted to finish hiking the Trail and went back the next year. I started from where I got off making it a section hike. I felt like a thru-hiker and conducted myself accordingly. I believe that if you have to rethink your goals and change a priority here and there it does not make a failed goal. It does not make you a failure. The failure is not trying to attain the goal at all."

Anne Mausolff, The Green Mountaineer, just desired to do it, to hike through different states and types of geological features, enjoy the views, and study the wildlife and wildflowers. "I wanted to be on my own and independent, feeling my own physical and mental strength."

Nancy Marth, Geo, wanted to learn more about her surroundings. "I wanted to learn more about myself as well as the geography, the terrain, plant, and animal life, and the people of Appalachia while experiencing it first hand. I did learn a lot from fellow hikers and their knowledge. I wish I could have carried books to read about the areas I was hiking through, but I always wanted to cut down on weight when I could. In the future, I would try to learn more about my surroundings and even carry a lightweight manual."

Many hikers have certain expectations of what a thru-hike will do for them as Cheryl Goudreau, Soulmates, suggests. "I felt that the Trail would make me see the changes in myself right away, but I found that they were very subtle, possibly because I was constantly looking within myself and trying to find how I was becoming a different person than when I first set foot on Springer Mountain. I thought that hiking for 6-7 months would give me the time to find a new direction for my life. I'd be able to decide what I wanted to do with the next 30-40 years that lay ahead. That 'revelation' never happened, probably because deep down inside I knew I would return to my home in Massachusetts and settle back down into the life I left behind."

Why People Do Not Finish

The vast majority of hikers, men and women, intending on completing a thru-hike do not fulfill their goal. For those hiking a traditional thru-hike, passing every white blaze with a pack on their backs from one terminus of the Appalachian Trail to the other in one continuous journey, the numbers drop drastically even further.

Hikers find certain conditions and situations demoralizing. Personal injury, illness, finances, weather, and homesickness can cause hikers to leave the Trail. One woman wrote that she couldn't eat sufficiently to keep energy levels high enough. Several left the Trail because of the illness or injury of a partner and didn't want to continue without them. Running out of time and needing to get back to school are reasons for some.

Only one woman who responded to the survey left the Trail in '96 because of the murders of two women near the Trail. Another writes, "Very few women don't finish the Trail because of safety concerns. They don't finish for many of the same reasons that male thru-hikers don't: lack of preparation, injury, goal changes, and external happenings." One said she was too slow, another got hypothermia, and one woman couldn't stand the bugs. A hiker who has made two attempts to thru-hike got off the first time because of illness, and the second time she just quit. Losing enthusiasm and feeling guilty for being away too long were other reasons. Dania Egedi, Lightweight, completed her '91 thru-hike but states, "Hiking the Trail turns into a job. You get up in the morning, hike all day, go to sleep at night. Yes, it may be a job you love, but six months of it makes it into a job. This is the mentally tough part of the hike."

Shari Galvez, Second Chance, thru-hiked in '98 but did not complete the Trail. She suggests there may be something missing in the literature about thru-hiking preparation despite the wide variety of readily available resources. "While doing my pre-hike research, a voice that was very absent was that of the majority of those who start a thru-hike: the 80-90% of those who do not complete all 2,160+ miles. Surely they must have something to say. And yet, they were nowhere to be found. While contemplating my departure from the Trail, I spoke with a man who was in the midst of his third thru-hike. I mentioned to him that he must have seen a lot of people trying to make the decision to stop hiking. He replied that wasn't true, that most would just slink away."

"Setting a goal, changing the goal, modifying the goal, achieving the goal, or discarding the goal is all one's choice. The silent voice of the hiker who starts at one end and doesn't get to the other end in one season is one I'd like to hear from more often. After all, we are of the majority. Did I reach Katahdin from Springer in one continuous hike? No. Was I successful in my thru-hike attempt? YES! I am proud of those miles. I risked things, saw things, learned things, became involved in a lifestyle that I never would have done otherwise."

"Those that complete 2160+ miles in one continuous journey have set a difficult course for themselves. I applaud their every step if that journey has helped them meet their goals. Perhaps we've all heard of some repeat thru-hikers who say that this time they want to do it differently. Somehow their first journey didn't fulfill them in the manner they had hoped. They learned from their first thru-hike how to enjoy it more on their second one. They changed their priorities. The task then becomes one of helping everyone who undertakes this challenge to feel like a success, whether it be injury, homesickness, discomfort, problems on the homefront or another adventure waiting that takes them from a planned thru-hike."

Cheryl Goudreau, Soulmates, intended to thru-hike as a purist following every white blaze along the AT. "The bad weather we encountered and an injury on day two made being a purist unrealistic for me. I do not feel like a failure just because I didn't achieve what I set out to do. I was able to hike from late February to early September and enjoy whatever came my way. I managed to hike 1700-1800 miles this year and am very happy with what I accomplished. I changed my focus from hiking from Georgia to Maine to just hiking to the next town."

"It's not fair to yourself to set monumental goals that seem so far off in the future. I learned that by setting small goals, then gradually increasing what I expected of myself, I did much better. I'd tell myself that I'd hike to the next shelter, see how I felt, and continue if I wanted to. The only pressure on me was self-induced and I learned when to increase and when to decrease that pressure. I learned to deal with obstacles in a more positive manner while hiking, and I feel that that has carried over into my post-hike life."

Another multiple time thru-hiker suggests that hikers leaving the Trail don't want to be convinced to stay. They don't want to be encouraged. Their minds are made up so they leave with as little fuss as possible. Do these hikers show up at important Trail functions and social gatherings? That might depend on the reason they left the Trail. If not completing their hike gave them a sense of failure, they might not want to associate with 2000 milers who are not shy about expressing pride in their accomplishment.

Sarah Dixon wanted to hike the Trail and see all that it had to offer and do it before the snow flew in Maine. "I wasn't particular about doing it in so many months or hiking so many miles a day. I just wanted to enjoy myself. I was unable to do that the first two times. Now I just want to go back. If it takes me until I'm 60, so be it. Actually I think if I finished it all at one time, I wouldn't have a good excuse to go back. I don't think I'll ever be able to get enough of the AT. It used to mean a lot to be a 2000 miler and now it doesn't seem so important. What makes up a 2000 mile hike is what is important."

Christine Shaw, Firefly, a '96 thru-hiker, related her experience through the on-line listserve. "I think it is important that when you ask someone why they didn't finish the Trail, every person will give you a different answer. Of the people who did finish, it seemed that physical preparation and gear didn't really matter. Some people were old, some were young, some were out of shape, and some went to great lengths to get in shape before the hike. Some had top of the line gear and spent lots of money; some had stuff from their garage. Some didn't speak English when they started but did when they finished. Some had extensive wilderness and backpacking experience, and some had never put a backpack on until Springer."

"On my first night on the Trail there were 24 people at the shelter and we sat around and discussed that 10% success rate issue. I really don't believe you can look at someone and know whether they are going to finish or not, though some people claim you can tell. You would have to know what was going on in their heads to figure that out. Of those 24 people, many of them did hang on for a really long time. I attribute part of that to us being early starters and having really bad snow. After a while the bad weather did not phase us much, and we were perhaps a bit more toughened to it than later starters. In the end, four of us finished. Two were husband and wife with extensive wilderness experience. A third was an early twenties go with the flow kind of guy who was a paddler by nature. I was the fourth, and I was certainly not one they would have picked based on first day impressions! I have since seen some of them again, and they told me they figured I would only last a week or two."

Christine says that the only thing that really took her by surprise was the pain of the trip. "I didn't expect there to be so much pain. I hadn't really considered the issue until I was knee deep in it. Unless you are some kind of superhuman, your body isn't going to like this hike thing at first. It will take a long time to adjust to 8-12 hours of exercise a day. Blisters, chaffing, shin splints, broken bones, knee problems, back problems, foot problems, sunburn, frostbite, hypothermia, heat exhaustion, malnutrition, diarrhea, giardia, lyme disease, severe weight loss, cuts, bruises, etc. That is a lot to deal with all at once. Well, maybe not ALL at once, but you get the picture. It is definitely more than your usual day of aches and pains."

A '97 thru-hiker, suggests that it's the discomfort factor that sends people home. "A lot of injuries heal with time or just require you to slow down a bit. Many people who say they had an injury derail their hike and don't come back even when they can. Maybe they weren't being honest with themselves as to why they left the Trail."

"In truth, it doesn't really matter why. If they hated every minute of their hike, then they made the right decision to leave. Granted, it's a lot easier to say that an injury sent you home than to admit that you were just tired of it all, but I think the mental stuff sends people home much more often than any other type of injury."

Writing from the Trail, a hiker who later left laments, "Many people repeatedly say they love it out here. I'm confessing I do not love it. Too much of it...the long-distance hiking and the camping and the town resupplying...are new to me and not second nature. I wonder when the joys of 'living in nature' and the moments of spirituality will manifest. Right now each action seems to take all of my thoughts. The walking is like work. Much of the same old same old...dirt, rocks, gravel, dirt, leaves, mud."

Sometimes an individual's personal journey and quest for growth may need to take a different route. Thru-hiking the Appalachian Trail is an exercise in commitment. A woman must be willing to pay the price. Motivation is intrinsic, and no one but the hiker herself is responsible for whatever feelings of success or failure she may have whether she completes the hike or not.

What is the relationship between hiking and self-image? What weight changes and muscle development can be expected?

Women both lost and gained weight throughout the course of their thru-hikes. This often depended on their particular body make-up before the hike. They were eager to report on this most sensitive of subjects and on how hiking effects their body image.

Section hiker, Jane Marriott, Pokey, wrote, "I have never met a female that felt OK about her body. If our hair looks great today, then there is always that 'pooch' or cellulite or wrinkle. The models put in front of us from birth were never real women. They were mutant females resembling junior high school boys. Their personal accomplishments and intelligence were of no matter. These were our role models, put in front of us by men and the media. Being who we are as women, we followed, and built our individual images of ourselves based on those standards. What a mess. Hiking the Trail changed my image of myself. I still deal with the world image, but when I got off the Trail and plopped down in my former surroundings, I found that I carried myself differently. My body was powerful. It was able to do things I never thought it could. I could work past the pain and strain to new levels. I could hike miles and miles and every mile felt better and better. Yeah, I still had short thick legs and a pear shaped ass, but it was not a source of shame for me. I did not feel like I should somehow apologize for my body. My body was wonderful; it was my friend! I was so much more physical, free, and peaceful about myself."

"Now that I have been off the Trail for a while all that is waning. I need another fix. I remember my friend and I were taking 'bird baths' in the middle of gorgeous pristine forest surroundings. Neither one of us felt at all self-conscious about our female bodies. We were just a part of all the other natural things around us. We had to take deliberate measures to carefully fuel and care for those bodies. They were not our enemies that had betrayed us with imperfections…Ah, what good times. When we got back, we both commented that we 'used' our bodies differently. We were more confident and open sexually. We were not 'hung up' on food; food was our friend, not our dreaded enemy. We 'felt forward-like' rather than hesitant. We felt empowered."

Beverly Hugo, Maine Rose, had lost so much weight by the time she got to New Hampshire and the White Mountains she could feel a lump under the skin on one of her hips. "I immediately started planning my funeral. Two day hikers I met on a stressful descent from Mausilauke gave me a lift to a clinic in town. It was out of their way, but I simply told them I needed their help. The doctor said it was just a fat deposit that had probably been there all along and I just hadn't been able to feel it!"

"A year later I was called back after a routine mammogram. The radiologist saw calcifications. I visualized my summit climb of Katahdin

126

during the biopsy. Whatever the result I told myself I would get through it just as I had the really tough times on the Trail; the miles and miles of ridge walk outside of Bland alone in a lightning storm; another solo from Grafton Notch to Frye Notch lean-to in treacherous weather. On leaving the office, they handed me a red rose. How appropriate I mused. A few days later I got a call from the nurse. It was malignant. She felt terrible and said she felt as if she was the grinch who stole Christmas. I told her not to worry. I'm Jewish."

"I was lucky. Four days later I was in surgery for a lumpectomy and there were clean margins around the area of the calcifications. No radiation or chemo was necessary. Throughout those weeks I managed to stay calm and focused on the strengths I had gained from my thru-hike."

Other women take up hiking after mastectomies expressing the confidence that hiking and backpacking helps restore a positive self-image. Future thru-hiker, Kathy Britt, writes, "I am 31 years old now. In 1996, at age 29, I was diagnosed with breast cancer. I thought I was going to die immediately. Fortunately, I'm still around. I had just recently started dating the woman who is now my partner. The day I found out, we packed our bags and headed for the mountains the next morning. My friend's parents had a cabin near Helen, Georgia where we stayed and did lots of soul searching. After two days, we decided to take a short day hike on the AT. I'm not even sure what section we hiked, but we did a few miles. Neither one of us had ever talked to the other about hiking, but we found that we were great companions on the Trail."

"On the drive back to Atlanta, we decided then that we would thru-hike the Trail someday. This decision gave me a goal, an event in the future to anticipate. The whole two hour drive back, that's all we talked about. I spent many an hour in the hospital (mastectomy), chemo room and hospital again (bone marrow transplant) reading books and doing research on thru-hiking. I cannot begin to explain how much the goal of thru-hiking helped my state of mind. By giving me a goal for the future and something to occupy my mind during those many torturous months, planning a thru-hike helped keep me focused and gave me a very positive outlook."

"Now, a couple of years later, we are making definite plans for a thru-hike in 2000. We go to the mountains and to the Trail as often as possible but only for short trips. My hike will begin almost exactly four years to the date of when I was diagnosed. I can't think of a better way to celebrate my life." Kathy has since had surgery to remove her ovaries, uterus, other breast, along with a bonus appendectomy! She was able to go for short walks after two weeks. She feels better than she has for years, both mentally and physically, and her thru-hiking plans are well underway.

Women thru-hikers add their comments
about weight loss and muscle development

"I lost 25 pounds before getting to Damascus. I think I could stand to lose that weight. I weigh as much now as I did when I completed the Trail and feel great."

"I lost two pounds on my hike; essentially my weight didn't change. I ate well and lost fat and gained muscle. I finished in much better shape than I start."

"Both my husband and I started the hikes with trim figures. I lost 11 pounds and he lost 22. Two years post hike, he has gained back 21. I gained back 15 and now battle to keep my weight down. My legs have developed varicose veins and my thighs rub together when I walk. I had none of these before the hike."

"I developed big leg muscles. I didn't have substantial leg muscles before I started my thru-hike and at the end I had large and defined legs. Compared to the guys' legs, my legs weren't that muscle bound."

"I actually ended the Trail weighing one pound more because I gained muscle mass. My percentage of body fat was very low to begin with so I didn't have much to lose or to draw from during my hike. I definitely had well defined calf and thigh muscles but far from bulging."

"I lost a lot of weight, about 20 pounds. I didn't realize I had that much to lose. The women I hiked with lost less weight than the guys did, but we were all tying our pants up with rope! Some of us lost weight in our breasts and some didn't."

"I lost a lot of fat in my breasts and became rather flat chested. My body cannibalized the fatty stores in my breasts during the hike when I didn't eat enough calories to sustain the activity. I was rather fit when I started the Trail so there wasn't much fat to burn. Happily after my hike, I regained my breast size due to more reasonable eating habits and lowered activity."

"I lost 25 pounds on the Trail. My cup size decreased two sizes. I was in good shape when I started and just became leaner. My legs became very muscular especially my calves."

"I lost a total of 8 pounds. It is almost impossible to eat the amount of calories needed to match the energy output, so one is typically going to lose weight."

Kelly Winters, Amazin' Grace, gained 12 pounds on the hike, all muscle. "If you're small to begin with, you'll lose what little fat you have and gain the muscle you need to hike. If you have extra fat and enough muscle, you'll lose the fat and hone the muscle. If you have a lot of extra fat, say goodbye to it. Try to lose as much of it as possible before the hike, because the extra weight will make hiking difficult. You won't get 'big' muscles like a man from hiking; women don't have the hormones for that. You will look fabulous though by the time you reach Maine."

"Most of the women I met on the Trail did not have significant weight change. I lost 4 pounds. The weight change is misleading, however, because my body composition changed dramatically. Much of my fat disappeared and was replaced with muscle. I went down a pants size and looked much more fit."

Rachel Dubois, Solophile, '97 came off the Trail weighing 10 pounds more than when she started. "I was in decent shape when I began the Trail and pretty happy with my weight. About a month or two into the Trail I found a scale and was heartbroken to see that after having walked hundreds of miles, I had actually gained weight! It took me a while to adjust my mindset. I had to re-teach myself not to look at the scale, but to look at my body and how I felt. My legs were much firmer and more muscular and there was no doubt that my energy and endurance were at all time highs in my life. What difference should it make that I weighed more? I think the gain in weight is a fairly common thing in women, unless you started the Trail overweight. I don't think the Trail should be looked at as a means of weight reduction, but rather as a way to really get in shape and develop a sense of physical confidence that you may have never experienced before."

"I lost about 40 pounds and at times ate a lot! When I first started in Georgia, I never seemed to be hungry. I was carrying around all this food and didn't want to eat it. I think I had a touch of altitude sickness, nausea and some dizziness, and headaches. After I adjusted, it seemed I could not get enough to eat. I was working off the calories I was consuming and didn't lose muscle tone. If anything I gained useful muscles." After her hike, this woman has since found she has very high blood pressure, possibly a condition that existed while hiking, and now takes daily medication.

"I lost over 50 pounds and regained it all plus more. I found it difficult to stay motivated to work out for the time and intensity necessary to maintain such a loss. I am, despite the weight gain, more at peace with my body now."

What benefits can women expect from hiking the Trail?

Dot MacDonald, D-Train, feels the benefits of thru-hiking transcend gender. "To walk and look and see what you see, to reflect, to be a pilgrim. To learn to accept others for who they are, not what they do or how they dress, or even what others think of them. To throw yourself onto the kindness of others, to trust. To forget that there are any differences between us if only for a few minutes through some magical shared time. And to do it for a long time. What a privilege and what an opportunity. The goodies for us as women are all the icing on that cake."

"Hiking has helped me test my limits," adds Dot's sister Barbara DiGiovanni, D-Boss. "In the world I grew up in there was no need to test limits. I had an overprotective mother and father. I was loved, encouraged to succeed in school, shuttled around, overindulged and happy that way. Sports for girls were not encouraged in the 50's and 60's. It was the odd woman who seriously participated in sports of any kind."

"Fortunately for me my sister was one of those people. She excelled in anything she attempted. When we started to hike she made me push past my limits. She helped me realize my physical capabilities. The Trail was the testing ground for me. I learned there was little I couldn't do if I could hike 20 or 30 miles on a weekend or four day holiday. My confidence in myself grew. It extended to my job, marriage, and personal relationships. I gained a better self-image. I cared less about what people thought of me and re-evaluated my relationships with my friends. I gained a clearer view of my place in the cosmos. Maturity also had a lot to do with this, but hiking started the ball rolling."

"One benefit is developing a greater sense of self-efficiency," says Dania Egedi, Lightweight. "Being in great shape. Mental toughness. A certainty that you can handle what life gives you. Friendships that last. I feel that I have deeper resources to draw from, physically and mentally. Sometimes, if people are treating me like I don't count, and as though I am somehow less than they are, I remember hiking the Trail. I stand a little taller and with a little more confidence. I think how I have accomplished something that they would never dream of doing."

Anne Mausolff, The Green Mountaineer, had improved eyesight after her hike and, of course, physical fitness. "A woman has increased self-sufficiency and independence, and a deeper, different awareness of life and what is essential. There is increased self-awareness and understanding as well. A woman can learn to listen better to her inner, true self. Experiencing what it is to do something simply because one wants to, not for any social or familial 'should' or expectations is a prime benefit of thru-hiking the Trail."

Section hiker, Diane Kortan, describes herself as a shy person, ill at ease in a group of strangers. "All this changed one evening around the campfire at a shelter filled with Boy Scouts and their leaders. Somehow, I found myself the center of attention, the whole conversation directed to me, everyone hanging on my every word. I talked on and on about my adventures and they all wanted to hear more. They were interested in my 'bravery', I felt confident and ebullient. My exploits really did sound fascinating and unusual, I must admit. I came across as rather an

131

extraordinary woman. The experience has given me a tremendous boost to my self-confidence." Diane recently took that new found confidence with her as she hiked glaciers in New Zealand and took a dive course off the Great Barrier Reef in Australia.

Family nurse practitioner and mother of a three year old and newborn, Judy Gallant Root, J-Walker, took time out of her very busy schedule to share some personal insights. "At many difficult times in my life since the Trail, I have reflected on my experiences and have told myself, 'you can do it.' There were physical and emotional hardships like crossing the Kennebec (not in the canoe), overcoming my aversion to putting my warm dry feet in those cold, wet leather boots one more rainy morning, or swallowing down another Lipton dinner because that was all I had, or continuing the hike with a strained knee ligament with 400 miles to go. My attitude over the years has been, 'if I could do that, I can do anything!' Anything has included going to grad school full-time and living apart from my husband for 18 months, living in Colorado to do migrant nursing, and becoming a mother."

Joyce Scott, Poor Nameless Hiker, stresses that "backpacking has taught me I am equal to males and I am only a victim to limitations and stereotypes if I allow myself to be. My thru-hike specifically taught me to love my body as my friend and partner. When I finally gazed upon Katahdin, I patted my thighs which have been the bane of my existence since junior high and said, 'good thighs. You carried me 2000 miles. Thank you'."

"The strongest benefit I have received as a female backpacker is the sense of belonging to something greater than myself. I think women are able to 'tune in' to the rhythm of nature easier than men. I can't say much more about the sensation; you have to experience it to understand it, but I can tell you, it has changed who I am completely."

Lisa Price, The Three Amigos, has been a reporter and is now a freelance writer. She loves archery hunting, is a columnist for Bow & Arrow Hunting and The Maine Sportsman, and has been published in a number of other magazines. The author met Lisa who was instructing a target archery class at a Becoming an Outdoors Woman weekend in Maine.

This past year Lisa shot a bear with her bow during bow hunting season in Maine. "In a way, and I know this will sound strange, the acts of drawing a bow on an animal and climbing a mountain have similarities. In each, there must be something inside that keeps you focused. When I'm about to let an arrow go, there are hours of practice behind the shot, and knowing this helps me keep my senses, even though my heart is pounding. When you're working to a summit, and more summits day after day, there has to be something inside that you draw on to keep you going. The more miles you go, the more you come to know this strength in yourself and the integrity at your core. I'm also in touch with this strength and integrity when my bow is at full draw. But unless you've put the time in, in both sports, that feeling is missing. After the 'kill' or after the summit, the feelings are still similar. A great memory, a trust in yourself, a little regret and the desire to do it again. So...the ultimate trip....backpacking and tenting out, on a hunting trip!"

The AT Thru-Hike as a Pilgrimage

In the middle of compiling this book, the author was on a plane to Phoenix perusing U.S. Air's in-flight magazine. The whole issue was devoted to pilgrimages in exotic locations all over the world. "Pilgrimages permeate all history and cultures, you would almost think that spiritual wanderlust is hard-wired into the human psyche. To this day journeys of meaning occupy millions of seekers. Pilgrims will be marching on dauntless at the turn of the millennium-an excuse by itself for meaningful meandering (Time Marches, US Airways Attache, July 1998, p.66)."

An Appalachian Trail thru-hike has all the prerequisites of an American pilgrimage, if the individual hiker desires a meaningful spiritual experience. An awareness that this is indeed possible may serve a prospective thru-hiker by helping her make certain choices along the way that may influence the depth a thru-hike can offer.

133

Kelly Winters, Amazin' Grace, hiked in '96 when she was 33. "I didn't know about the Trail until '94 when I saw a book about it, but I knew it was the pilgrimage I had been looking for. I was right! I hiked 1000 miles alone, and then hooked up with a trail buddy, also female, for most of the rest. It was an incredible experience."

KELLY'S PILGRIMAGE

I did this trek because my life was not working. I was confused, had been in some unsuccessful relationships that only confused me more, and did not know what to do for a career. I had spent years wandering around, doing temp jobs, moving from city to city. It's a common way of life among people in their 20's and 30's these days, but not a very productive one, and not a very happy one.

I felt there was a "place" I needed to reach: not a physical place, but an emotional, psychological, spiritual one. And although the place was not physical, somehow I knew the only way to get there was to physically walk a great distance, a long arduous process. A pilgrimage. I didn't know what the place was or what I would find there, but I trusted that it existed and it was reachable. And I knew that it was as necessary as blood or breath. When I heard about the Trail, I knew it was the Long Walk I needed.

Out there hiking, or standing at the edge of the road thumbing a ride to some small town so I could resupply, I felt what the writer Natalie Goldberg describes as "Great Determination." She quotes her Zen Buddist mentor, Katagiri Roshi, who told her, "Your little will can't do anything. It takes Great Determination. Great Determination doesn't mean just you making an effort. It means the whole universe is behind you and with you-the birds, trees, sky, moon, and ten directions."

This is how I felt on the trip and it was a gift, something I had not earned, a journey given to me for reasons I did not understand, but that I trusted. I believed in the absolute necessity of what I was doing. If I quit before reaching the place I needed to get to, wherever and whatever it might be, I would have to keep coming back until I completed the task I had been given. I felt, simply, blessed to be there, doing the work, doing the walk.

It worked. By the time I reached New England I had changed deeply. I had outwalked the old burdens, hurts, fears, and confusions that seemed to make my load so heavy in the first part of the trip. Every mountain I walked over had become a part of me; I felt wider and deeper, with a groundedness no one could ever take away. I had endured months of physical hardship, had trusted thousands of strangers and been rewarded with nothing but help and kindness. I had outwalked the horizon more times than I could count. I would never feel the same limitations I'd felt before. I knew what I wanted in life.

Everything I'm doing now is a direct result of the walk. I met my life partner on the Trail and chose to move to New York, which I love, to be with her. Because of the trip, when I returned to civilization, I found the courage to start my own successful business. My partner and I bought a house, an unimaginable thing during my unsettled, rootless life before the Trail. My relationship with my family has changed and grown deeper. I'm happy.

I realize now that all my wandering was because I hadn't found the life I needed. It's easy to be dedicated, stable, and grounded if you're doing what's right for you. Or if, in too many cases, you're secretly afraid you haven't found your true life, you can't bear to take the risk of losing the half-life you have. Fear keeps more people in one place than happiness, because sometimes finding happiness requires taking some risks. If you are like that, I want to encourage you to take that risk. Give your heart to the path, and beauty will come.

Life after the Trail

Asha Williams, Footprints, struggled with adjustment a few months after completing her '97 thru-hike. "People want to know what was the hardest part of the Trail. My answer surprises my colleagues. The hardest part is life after the Trail. Life was easier when I carried everything I needed on my back, and when all I desired was the beauty and companionship that already surrounded me. Off the Trail it is harder to walk down life's path without the 2x6 inch white blazes to guide me."

" I am still trying to readjust. For over six months the Trail was my life. Suddenly it is gone. Now there is this huge hole in my life. I am struggling with putting my life back together again and finding a way to fill that hole. I spent the first three months after the Trail sleeping on the porch in my sleeping bag. I continue to keep all my toiletries in a Ziploc bag and literally licked my bowl clean to make it easier to wash the dish. I have my toothbrush in a holder in the bathroom now. I believe I once again have normal table manners and have finally advanced to sleeping in my bed with the sleeping bag as a blanket. Maybe eventually I will graduate to using sheets and a bedspread."

"I experience flashbacks daily. One minute I am shopping for dinner, the next moment I am walking down the Trail with little spring flowers at my feet. Going up the stairs to my apartment I imagine a heavy pack on my pack. Suddenly I am climbing up White Cap Mountain with winds at 60 miles an hour and hail hitting me on the face. So much of daily life seems frivolous and superficial off the Trail. It is all so fast paced. I miss the mountains. I miss watching vultures soar across the sky and feeling the earth beneath my feet. I miss a life where with every person on the Trail I share an unspoken but undeniable bond, and with everyone I meet I can immediately call 'my friend.' Walking all 2160.2 miles of the Appalachian Trail is, without question, the greatest experience of my life."

Dania Egedi, Lightweight, had difficulties adapting back to society after the Trail. "Everything moved too fast. Cars scared me. I went long periods of time on the Trail without talking, and I had a hard time expressing myself or thinking of certain words. I got tired of my inability to express the Trail experience. I started resorting to stock answers and was very disappointed in myself. I still had my trail appetite but not the physical exercise. I knew about the tendency of thru-hikers to pack on weight after the Trail, but it was very hard not to overeat. I took a temporary job after the Trail to make some money until I could find a 'real' job, and spent lots of afternoons crying, depressed with my life. Physically, my feet were so tender for weeks that I could hardly walk."

Kirsten Lincoln, like Asha, feels her hike was by far the greatest experience of her life. "I learned a lot about myself and about a cool way to live, enjoying life and living in the moment." Kirsten brings her new perspective on how to be happy to a wilderness experiential learning camp for troubled youth. Hope Smith expresses the sentiment that she, at last, had a true adventure and tourist-type travel no longer has appeal. Cindy Miller, Mrs. Gorp, writes, "I have strength in the knowledge that I can accomplish that which I set out to do...but once a thru-hiker, always a thru-hiker. There are more trails out there to hike...and I will."

A '96 hiker struggled with depression on completing her thru-hike. "Many of the thru-hikers I knew went through some form of depression after hiking the Trail. I heard that this would happen but was so sure it wouldn't happen to me. When many of the thru hikers I knew finished, they had to find a place to live and a job. I had my spouse waiting for me at home and didn't have to work. Still, depression hit."

" Wingfoot told me that a thru hike of the AT is usually a time of transition. At the time of my hike I didn't know this. But looking back I can see what a time of change in my life it was. My children were growing up, forcing me to decide what I was going to do with the rest of my life. And I also had more time to spend with my husband with whom I had very little in common. I had to accept that I was no longer a mother with young children and move on to something else. Then my husband and I had to work on finding common ground. I am now back in college excited about a new career as an elementary school teacher. My husband and I joined a local running club and are currently training for a marathon. Focusing on these new goals has helped give my life new meaning."

Depression also hit another '96 2000 miler, Lisa Groshong. "I had read that some thru-hikers get depressed after coming off the trail, and I didn't really believe it. After all, I was headed home to a reunion with my partner and I'd been homesick for months dreaming of being home. But I got slammed with depression that lasted a really long time. Mostly, I think it was due to not exercising, being cooped up in a house, having extremely unrealistic expectations of how great it would be to be home, and losing the

Trail community, running into pals on a daily basis. So I would recommend that a woman hiking the Trail have a plan for when she gets home, something to keep occupied and engaged in the world so you don't withdraw."

Cheryl Goudreau, Soulmates, finds it very hard to talk about the impact of her '98 thru-hike. "I find it difficult to find the words to describe how hiking for 6-7 months through all kinds of weather, meeting incredible people in towns and on the Trail, and actually living my dream has affected me. I do know that when you climb Mt. Katahdin (or Springer Mountain if you go southbound), the journey does not end when you reach that final blaze. The journey continues on a different level. The many days of hiking on the AT are etched deeply within my heart and will be with me forever."

"I did find the return to my 'other life' was easier than expected. My husband and I spent a lot of time in the towns we passed through during our hike because we enjoyed the little luxuries that these towns offered…restaurant food, a laundromat, a hot shower. I took a month off between summiting Mt. Katahdin and returning to work which was perfect for me. I had time to get my belongings moved into an apartment and time to just sit and reflect back on my time spent on the Trail."

"I did find, however, that my patience level dropped. Other hikers have told me that theirs increased, but I found myself becoming irritated with people who couldn't make quick decisions, who were afraid to pull out into traffic, etc. I do feel the every-day stresses faster than I used to, but find that if I take time in the evening and let my mind wander, I can 're-live' certain events in my hike that were very enjoyable, thereby relieving the stress I'm feeling."

"Instead of purchasing a second car when we returned, we found an apartment in the city about a half mile from my office. I now walk to work each day, even in the bitter cold of winter, and feel good that I'm still 'hiking' every day. I get a little exercise, fresh air, and time to unwind a bit after work. I also feel good about not contributing to the traffic jams and air pollution. When I do use the car to go shopping, I don't look for the closest place to park. I don't mind parking at the far end of a parking lot and walking more to get into the store. I guess after hiking 10-20 miles a day over difficult terrain, walking an extra 200 yards doesn't seem like such a big deal any more."

"I had a fairly rough adjustment period when I came off the Trail." a '97 hiker, took an additional six weeks off after summiting Katahdin to travel and visit family and friends. "When the day finally arrived when I was supposed to actually walk back through the doors of the company where I had gotten a leave of absence, I spent the day on the couch at home in tears. It was supposed to be different now. I wasn't supposed to end up in the same place that I was before I started the Trail. My world was supposed to be a different place; I NEEDED it to be a different place. And yet, there I was reporting back to the same company, living in the same city, filling my life up with the same meaningless things that drove me to hike the Trail in the first place."

"I struggled with that for several weeks. Around January or February things started to brighten for me. I realized that my physical surroundings might be the same as they were a year ago, but I had changed. It was a great revelation. I didn't need a new city or a different job to make me happy. I finally began to understand that it was me, my thoughts, my outlooks, and my plans that would make my life a happy one. I felt so liberated by this discovery. It was a bit slow in coming and it took a while to flesh itself out. I truly look at my life now and I'm very happy with it, because I am very happy with myself. I have so much optimism about my future. Come what may, my outlook is the key to it all. Everything is possible as long as I'm willing to allow myself to dream and have the courage to believe in me and my abilities to grab those dreams."

Carey Fields, Pennsylvania Rose, reflects on hiking young and unprepared. "I got a huge sense of self-esteem and ability to set priorities. Not much is as bad as hiking in 40 degree weather when it's raining, you're wearing jeans and inadequate rain gear, and it's two miles uphill to the nearest shelter. Not much is as important as food, water, clothing, heat, and love."

Two time thru-hiker, Ginny Owen, Spirit Walker, found her wings. "Successfully thru-hiking the AT did make a big difference in how I look at myself. I had lost confidence in my ability to achieve much of anything. I was a 31-year-old bookstore manager, stuck in a rut, and going nowhere. I started the Trail with no idea whether I could succeed. I only knew I had to try. When I realized halfway through Maine that I was going to reach Katahdin, I felt as if I had found my wings and could once again fly. I saw the limits I had placed around my growth and achievement were self-imposed. I could do anything I really wanted, if I was willing to pay the price whatever that turned out to be. Sometimes the price is higher than I am willing to pay. I still place boxes around myself, but I also know they are self-imposed and temporary. That 'I can't' just means that I haven't tried yet."

A sense of independence and accomplishment, an appreciation of learning to deal with adversity, and a chance to live outside for six months are what, Carolyn Cunningham, Tawanda, feels are great benefits of thru-hiking the Trail. "I realize I was experiencing a way of life that included beautiful views, fresh air, and miles and miles of walking. It also included meeting people I never would have come in contact with off the Trail, forming intense friendships with people that continue to this day, and becoming part of a community of long-distance hikers that all see the world in a different way after hiking the Trail."

Lisa Barter, Tinkerbell, describes the essence of her experience. "While my ideas of fulfillment and happiness have not changed since I hiked the Trail, doing that hike gave me the courage to accept nothing less. I was completely unwilling to go back to a stressful job in a big polluted city, so I made some strong decisions that afforded me the opportunity to work and live in a much better environment. The Trail helped me to develop the courage to stand up for what's best in my life."

Verna Soule, Gran'ma Soule, feels very close to God on the Trail. "He has always been there for me. Sometimes I think I give him a hard time depending on him so much but I know he is always there."

Mary Sands, Mama Boots, feels the Trail and writing her book deepened her religious and spiritual life. "I felt it was a call from God to write the book as well as share my love of nature with the next generation."

Donna Savluk, Ward's Girl, relates a Trail experience that

impacted her spiritually. "On August 2, 1994, alone in a hailstorm above treeline, I tore a tendon in my ankle near Sphinx Col in the Presidentials. The specter of a guy named Jay, whom I met and camped with the very first time I nervously went backpacking alone, appeared out of nowhere. The night we first met Jay told me about the Trail. I knew virtually nothing about it at the time. He had hiked a good chunk of the Trail and told me lots of stories about his hike and inspired me to hike the AT. Now his specter guided me down Caps Ridge Trail where a lone car, occupied by a sleeping rock climber named Mike, offered me a ride to the hospital. I never saw Jay again and even wonder if he was 'real' the first time we met."

"I believe that there was a stronger force that wanted me to complete this trip," writes Kathy Kelly Borowski. "Trail Magic was always there when I needed it. Although I could not finish the Trail in one year, I did have the opportunity and desire to keep going."

Nancy, Geo, Marth's brother died in September '96 the year before her thru-hike. "From Springer Mountain to Katahdin, I carried some of his ashes in a film canister. I really believe that he was watching over me and had something to do with my safe and successful journey. I never had any 'visits' from him while on the Trail, but I was sure he was with me at times. On September 7, 1997 one year from the day he died, I said a short prayer and spread some of his ashes on top of Carter Dome in New Hampshire, the highest point of my hike that day. On October 8 when I reached Baxter Peak, I took out the canister and let the wind carry the rest of his ashes. Reflecting since then, I think it was a significant step in the process of closure."

Beverly Hugo, Maine Rose, felt the power of the white blazes at an art exhibit the winter after her hike. "I took my teenage daughter to see a one man show of woodsy nature paintings by a man from a local hiking club. In only one picture and in only one instance was there a man made 'object' in a painting, a white blaze on a tree. With my daughter slightly embarrassed at my side, I stood there overcome with emotion as the tears streamed down my face. Even though I had been showing my AT slides on a regular basis, seeing the white blaze so unexpectedly only intensified the whole experience for me."

Women & Thru-Hiking on the Appalachian Trail

Melody Blaney, Midnite, has always had a deep Christian belief but felt a presence of God she had never experienced. "After a nasty fall on wet rocks in New York, I was left with minor physical injuries but mentally scarred for the rest of my hike. One particular day after my fall, it began to rain as I approached a large boulder field and I could feel the anxiety and fear well up inside. I fought back the tears and suddenly the words, 'Fear not for Thou art with Thee' came into my head and a calm spread over my entire body that stayed with me whenever I repeated those words."

"I am not a religious person and never have been," writes Sarah Dixon. "I truly found my spirituality on the Trail though. I always thought myself to be a spiritual person but while hiking the Trail I was able to truly know what it means to be so. There is so much beauty and peace and time to reflect and ponder that it just kind of jumps out at you!"

Barbara DiGiovanni, D-Boss, feels that nature is certainly a place where you can meditate and pray easily. "The solitude in the woods is inspiring. I've met some of the most incredible people over the years and miles who have humbled me in their faith in God and who have shown me that indeed we find Him in every person we meet if we only look. The sweetest memory is of meeting two fellows on Mt. Horrid in Vermont singing hymns and playing guitar. My sister, husband, and I sat with them for a while and joined in singing 'Morning has Broken.' The view was never more spectacular and the feeling of oneness with God was really present with us."

Do you have a different perspective on life after thru-hiking the Trail?

"When I walked into my house after my thru-hike, I looked around at all my 'stuff' and couldn't believe all the things I had that I really didn't need," writes Regina Erskine, Whispering Pine. "We really can survive on very little and I think the more 'stuff' we have, the more we lose sight of what is important. Not only is this true with material things, but with the way we live our lives as well."

142

Women & Thru-Hiking on the Appalachian Trail

Rachel Dubois, Solophile, feels that many of the things about her day-to-day life may appear similar to the person she was before her thru-hike. "But I am vastly different on the inside. I have great plans for my life, and I think they are very achievable. The future is a wonderful horizon. I now watch myself pretty closely to make sure I don't get consumed by certain dangers that are fairly common traps in our society: materialism, greed, hunger for the American definition of 'success', the quest for more, more, more. All these are looming pitfalls that could spoil my dreams if I let them. I want to keep my eyes on the 'big picture', the things that are truly important to my inner happiness. That will always guide me in the right direction."

Anne Mausolff, The Green Mountaineer, simply states, "The essentials are what I carried on my back; all else is 'convenience' or even 'luxury'."

"The Trail, without a doubt, has totally changed my life," reports Melody Blaney, Midnite. "I realized during and after my hike how cluttered life can become with materialistic things in a very fast paced world. If I could live for six months with everything I needed on my back, I certainly don't need a lot now that I've returned to 'the other world.' I no longer take things for granted, like turning on a faucet or wasting water while it's on, and being warm and dry. I have a much deeper appreciation for all that nature has to offer: watching the sun set from my sleeping bag, awakening before the birds begin their morning concert, the clean, fresh feeling of the woods after a summer rain, and the raw power of a storm above treeline. I was blessed with the opportunity to experience all four seasons in 179 days of hiking."

Sarah Dixon feels the AT changed her on the inside and in her head. "I realized that life is so simple; we've just made it complicated. Materialism is something that is absent from Trail life but sickeningly prevalent in the real world. Being out there puts everything in perspective. It changes the way you set priorities and makes you realize how important relationships are because they will be gone tomorrow. Relish every small detail for those are the things that are significant in this life. Don't run past the glorious views because you've got to make your miles. Study them. Be grateful for them. The next few miles might be rough."

"There are no 'big deals' on the Trail and if there are, they seem so easy to solve. In the real world everything is a 'big deal' and such a major project to figure out. I often get lost in all the real world garbage and when I do, I try to think of life on the AT to bring me back. Life is so easy with cars and computers and microwaves. On the Trail you had to work for what you wanted and it felt good to do that work. The real world should be like that instead of expecting something for nothing and someone to do it for you."

Dania Egedi, Lightweight, learned that things usually work themselves out on their own and not to sweat the small stuff although that's still a hard one. "Life, like the Trail, can only be hiked one step at a time. Water is the most wonderful thing on this earth."

"I have a little broader perspective than when I left," explains Hilary Lang, Weatherwoman. "I'm better able to project into the future and analyze the possible long-term effects of my actions, rather than demanding instant gratification. I'm more discerning about what personality traits to look for in people whether they are friends or significant others. I enjoy the simple things much more now, because I take the time to stop and notice them. I'm more open to new experiences. The Trail, and the people on it, opened me up to living. I love living, and that includes the good and the bad. I love the Trail on both the sunny flat days and the up-and-down monsoon days. I'm more willing to take chances now. I'm getting ready to move to North Carolina, quite a change for me since I've lived in Connecticut for most of my life. Best of all, I recognize Trail magic now and believe me, it does happen in the real world, too. Most of us just take it for granted. My Trailname has rubbed off on me. I'm Weatherwoman on the Trail, so now I'm going back to school to be a weatherwoman off the Trail as well."

When Nancy Marth, Geo, was younger, she had trouble bringing an idea or plan to fruition. "As I've gotten older, I've been able to change this. But it wasn't until the end of my thru-hike that I realized, 'Wow! Look at this big thing that I was able to plan for so long and actually carry out successfully.' What a confidence booster. I realized while hiking the Trail that if I could do this, I could do A-N-Y-T-H-I-N-G."

Leslie Niederstadt, Annapurna, '96 2000 miler, shared some life's lessons from her thru-hike. "Hiking the Appalachian Trail from end to end taught me many lessons both as a woman and a human being. Of those there are two that have most affected my life: faith and goal setting. It was a leap of faith to believe that I could walk the Trail in its entirety in one season. Many naysayers reminded me of the challenges, 'Six months is a long time to do the same thing.' 'You'll hurt yourself or someone else will hurt you.' But somehow, for some reason, it was important enough for me to do it. I never once questioned my ability to finish. I knew I would. I believed in myself. I trusted myself. I had faith in myself."

"I say this because in other areas of life these three things, trust, faith and belief seem to elude me - but somehow with the Trail it came easily and fully. There was also the sidebar lesson to this one and that is the knowledge that 'things' in general will work out. It is not the end of the world if one doesn't make the post office by 12 noon on Saturday. There are always options and when one door closes another opens. We have choices that are sometimes difficult to see until another way is blocked. On the Trail this nugget of truth made itself evident time and again."

"The second lesson I learned was that of setting short term goals for the long term one. No where else in life has this lesson been so eloquently demonstrated. The obvious goal was Katahdin - but there were all those other daily goals that helped me reach the final one. Now in life, when faced with a seemingly daunting task, if I break it up into 15 mile a day increments and visualize all those shelters I will stay at along the way, it appears do-able and within my reach. All that is left than is to commit to it, have faith in the process and myself and JUST DO IT!"

Post-hike lifestyle changes

Many women made serious lifestyle changes after their thru-hikes. Couples reevaluated their life direction. Some women in a mid-life transition don't even need an extended thru-hike to make a major change.

"I read somewhere that the dreams of your twenties will haunt you

145

in your forties," writes section hiker, Linda Ivey, Mountain Mama. "I guess I was having a typical mid-life crisis when I discovered Mama Boots and called her. I believe that God sent her to me. Since my first hike, I quit my job, homeschooled a daughter, changed churches, and increased my volunteer activities. I dusted off the original values that got lost in the quest for material accomplishments and middle-class goals. I have a long way to go, but thinking about certain places on the Trail can bring almost instant peace and contentment. I think my blood pressure actually lowers. A few fellow hikers joke that the feeling hits us about the same time. We have a need, usually monthly, to replenish ourselves. Being on the Trail is like taking a deep breath after being under water for several minutes, and it continues to refocus my life."

A number of 2000 milers have taken their experience public, speaking to groups, showing their slides, and giving talks in their own communities, states, and throughout the country. Jean Deeds, Indiana Jean, does motivational speaking through "Stretch Your Limits", has written a book, produced a video, and leads women only hikes. Verna Soule, Gran'ma Soule, presents "Tales of the Trail" throughout Michigan. After her thru-hike, Illah Sink, Sunflower, along with husband, Jim, Two Look Slim, two of the hikers featured on the Trailside PBS TV program, were booked solid in churches and community groups near their hometown in Ohio.

Beverly Hugo, Maine Rose, also featured on the Trailside show, has developed AT/state studies curricula for public schools and homeschoolers and presents her inspirational programs to business, community, and women's groups throughout the country through her speaking business, "HIT THE TRAIL!" Rosie has also hosted her own local public access TV program, "Ramblin' with Maine Rose" and is producing a number of motivational audio and video tapes.

Kay Cutshall, The Old Gray Goose, speaks to local groups in her corner of Ohio. Author, Melody Blaney, Midnite, does motivational speaking through "If You Can Dream It-You Can Do It" and teams up with Kathy Kelly Borowski giving backpacking courses. Virginia Logue has written and co-authored many books with husband Frank. Leslie Clapp, appropriately named Flower Power after her extraordinary gardening abilities, has developed programs of both her AT and PCT (Pacific Crest Trail) thru-hikes showcasing her photography talents.

Authors also include '96 thru-hiker Adrienne Hall and Mary Twitty, who completed a nine-year section hike of the Trail. Cindy Ross has written a number of books alone and with her husband on all sorts of adventure experiences, some including her own children...and llamas! Another prolific writer, Karen Berger, has authored a number of books as well as articles for Backpacker magazine. Joyce Mailman, Espy, is a Maine Guide, speaks for the AMC- Appalachian Mountain Club, and leads hikes in New England. These women and many others have taken the power of their experience and shared it with others. They've honed their stories, improved their public speaking skills, and brought their love of the Trail to many who might never be able to take a step on the AT.

Donna Horn, '78, writes, "I've acted on my sense of adventure; I didn't sit around saying 'I wish' or 'someday.' I've accomplished something I set out to do, despite challenges and adversities along the way. It gave me a credential to do other things in my life. I've worked for the Appalachian Trail Conference and other Trail organizations and it helped move me out of a job rut towards things I prefer doing. I've learned and demonstrated commitment and dedication. Hiking the Trail wasn't just a vacation, as friends thought when I quit my job to do it. While I was out there, hiking the AT was my occupation, education, recreation, and socialization. Looking back, it was an important part of my life...and still is."

Kathy Kelly Borowski also expresses strong sentiments. "Thru-hiking changed my life. Many good things have come out of this experience; it was life shaping. I now look at life much differently. Some material things are no longer important to me. I know I can live a simple life. The friends I've gained are irreplaceable. It showed me that there is still good in the world."

"Without a doubt, thru-hiking was the most difficult, exciting, and glorious six months of my life to date." Melody Blaney, Midnite, simplified her life. "I gave up my 9-5 job, now work 14 hours a day for minimum wage and love every minute of it. I'm working close to the Trail in an environment where I'm the happiest and most comfortable."

Nancy Marth, Geo, realized after her thru-hike that she needed to redesign the logistics of her life. "After taking a few months off before trying to find work, I decided to accept a part-time job where I could work continuously for a length of time and then have several weeks or months off in between. I wanted to have more time off and take that time for backpacking trips whenever I could. Before I left for the Trail, I enjoyed day hiking and did so when I could, but it was never a priority during my 'off time.' Now that I've hiked the AT, I think about getting back on a trail, any trail any time that I have off. Hiking brings a serenity that I crave when I feel spirituality depleted."

"Hiking the AT has made an impact on what I want to do with my life, what I don't want to do, what I will do with my spare vacation time in the future, who I connect with, my physical condition, my mental state. Simply put, the AT experience has shown me the things that really matter in life: believing in oneself and helping others."

"As long as I'm doing from my deepest, inner self, life gets better every day." Anne Mausolff is now 75 years old and has "miles to go before I sleep." Since completing the Trail, she has retired from leading cross-country ski and bicycle tours. Anne has traveled to almost every state, taken up water color painting, renewed an interest in calligraphy, learned to telemark ski, hiked the 100 highest mountains in New England, skied on Denali, and spent two months hiking, canoeing, and backpacking in Alaska. And that's only a fraction of her active life!

Sue Freeman, Blueberry, found that people drift after the AT. "It's difficult to assimilate back into society. I thought I would return to my corporate executive job, but downsizing at my company made that not an option. It was just as well. I would have had a hard time fitting back in. Instead, my husband and I joined our love of hiking with our dream of starting our own business. We began our writing and self-publishing by putting out a book on hiking trails around our hometown. That has led to other books on hiking and biking, and we now actively recruit other authors of outdoor recreation books. Our book publishing business is growing, and

148

we can continue working together and being outdoors a lot. Of course, the money is no where near our previous level, but we sold our house and downshifted our expectations. We're happier now, living on much less income."

Did thru-hiking the AT fulfill your goals?

"Friends, family, and acquaintances always want to know what was the best part of thru-hiking the Appalachian Trail in its entirety," writes Asha Williams, Footprints, '97. "Perhaps they expect me to say the wildlife or the scenery or not working for six months. I always surprise them when I answer by saying the people. 'The people,' they repeat, as if by reiterating those two words they will somehow understand my reply. They fall silent as they search my eyes looking for some sort of explanation to my response. I don't know how to share the deepness of my feelings towards the friendships and experiences I gained."

"It had become a way of life. It was hard, but I loved my simple life out there on the Trail. Even when I was wet, cold, hungry, and miserable, I was still happy because I was doing something I really wanted to do. There was no other place in the entire world I wanted to be. I had the best and worst days of my life out on that Trail. I was really sad when it was over."

Future thru-hiker, Karen Bouknight has outlined her goals for her end-to-end adventure.

1. To test myself physically, mentally, and emotionally over an extended period of time, using the Trail as my proving ground
2. To know my creator more personally by immersing myself in His creation
3. To positively impact people along the Trail, both hikers and townspeople

Rachel Dubois, Solophile, is still amazed by it all when she looks back over her '97 thru-hike. "When people ask me questions about it, I feel as if I'm talking about somebody else. The more time passes since leaving the Trail, the more amazing it becomes in my mind. Sometimes I have to remind myself that it was in fact ME who walked from Georgia to Maine, and that I did have some amazing resources of inner strength that I hope to continue to draw upon in my life."

Dania Egedi, Lightweight, had wanted to hike the Trail for years, but never had the time. "After getting bounced around at graduate school for several years, I wanted to get back to something that I really enjoyed and try to refocus on what I wanted out of life. I wanted to finish, but that was not the end-all. I tried to keep my focus on what I was feeling that particular day, and not focus on getting to Maine. It is easy to fall into the 'View, schmoo, I gotta get to Maine' mentality and I tried hard not to let that happen. The Trail was much more of a social experience than I was expecting or wanting. If I were to do it over again, I would start as early (or even earlier) and try to stay ahead of the crowds. Or maybe hike it North to South (Motto: the few, the proud, the southbound!) I was hoping that it would help me figure out what I wanted out of life, and it didn't, but that was probably too much to expect anyway."

The year after her '91 thru-hike, Dania went to Delaware Water Gap for the weekend to visit a friend who was thru-hiking the Trail again. She met another hiker, Blister, at the hostel and made one of those Trail connections that happen from time to time. It sure beats the bar scene. He didn't get her phone number but tracked her down using her Trailname and the fact that she worked at a university in Pennsylvania. All things seem possible on the Trail. They eventually moved to Kentucky to manage a rafting business and got married in an outdoor ceremony. The day was cold and rainy and for the ceremony, Dania wore polypro as well as her hiking boots under her wedding dress!

It should be noted that the vast majority of thru-hikers start in Georgia for a very good reason. Although Katahdin officially opens May 15, there can be weeks of delay due to ice and snow on the mountain a fact that can greatly hamper a southbounder's schedule. The heavy rains of '98 caused many a southbounder to leave the Trail. Also, starting too early from down south, as many a hiker can tell you, can put you smack in the middle of snow, sleet, and cold.

150

What Does Hiking Mean to You?

Marcia Fairweather, Almost There, is one woman making her mark for social change. She has a goal to just get more African-Americans into the out-of-doors because she seldom saw them participating in activities she enjoyed. On a hike near Harper's Ferry, she stopped at the ATC headquarters and viewed the replica display of the entire Trail in the glass case. "It was a very peaceful feeling, yet strange because I was standing there visualizing myself walking along the AT and doing something like this had never entered my mind before." She has found that the interest in hiking by African-Americans was more than she had expected, especially with women. "I have come to realize that planning programs and getting people back to nature is part of the mission I am here to fulfill and am beginning to focus my career on activities in this area. The desire to do the AT has helped me in understanding my life purpose and getting back to what I feel is the true religion of the world which is based more on the caring and loving of nature."

For Anne Mausolff, The Green Mountaineer, "Thru-hiking was the first thing in my life I did solely and entirely because I wanted to and it pleased me to do so. I have several albums of photos, sketch books, poems, and copious diary notes."

A thru-hiker writes, "Self-esteem has always been a problem and continues to be. But when I talk of the AT and remember my times there, I am reminded that I did a great thing, me, on my own. It feels good to know that I can. I think the longer the time goes since hiking, the lower the self-esteem drops because I forget how challenging it really was. I am confident that I could do it tomorrow and get through the tough times like I did before."

Florida residents, the Mountain Marchin' Mamas, have been section hiking the AT annually since '78 and maintain a shelter on the Trail in North Carolina. Grace Tyner, Amazing Mama, started hiking when she was 50 and wrote an article in a 1995 issue of the ATC Trailway News describing other small groups of middle-aged women who see age as no barrier when facing extensive backpacking trips on the AT.

151

Women & Thru-Hiking on the Appalachian Trail

Mary Pfennig, Hoosier Mama, expresses bittersweet feelings about the '99 completion of the Mamas 22-year section hike. "Aside from my role as wife and mother, my association with the Mountain Marchin' Mamas and the Appalachian Trail has given me more challenge, more pain, more satisfaction, more danger, more comfort, and more beauty than any other. It has been a priceless learning experience. I have discovered my physical capabilities have often been tested. Thanks to our 26 hikes over the years, my confidence in myself has increased dramatically. The average middle-aged woman does not really know her abilities. I truly thank the MMM's and the AT for allowing me to discover mine." Many a hiker has been serenaded on the Trail by the Mamas singing, "Happy Trails To You," as they passed in the opposite direction.

Another of the Mamas, Bunny Schneider, Mother Superior, credits their successful 26 hikes over 22 years to good planning, self-sufficiency, and fairness. "My husband, Jack, is our Trail Agent, carefully planning each trip for us. He researches the AT maps and guides for the section we will be hiking, locates all water sources, calculates hiking times, notes the terrain, and makes detailed annotated maps for each Mama. Each Mama is totally self-sufficient with regard to supplies but totally supportive of each other. We rotate the leader job daily and come to each hike with three lectures in mind. These always include 'The State of the Family Address' as well as topics covering history, household tips, and book reviews. There is absolutely no competition among us other than trying to have the lightest pack possible, or for a few of us, the heaviest. We have all the support and encouragement of our families and we are committed to finishing the Trail together."

Bunny is an educator, like several of the other Mamas, and works with hearing impaired high school students. Our survey indicated that 73% of 2000 milers surveyed are college graduates. Other Mamas include Ellen Kilpatrick, Charme Burns, and Sylvia Crump.

Future thru-hiker, Cheryl Hoovers, found her summer filled with working and hiking, working and hiking. Once, between weekend hikes and after 43 days of this routine, she placed her pack on her bed intending to move it but fell asleep. She woke in the morning with her arms around her pack dreaming she was back at the shelter. If this happens to a summer weekend AT hiker, imagine the dreams a thru-hiker must have!

Jean Arthur expresses enthusiasm for her life associated with the Trail and all the wonderful people she has met. She and her husband have attended AT conferences, ALDHA meetings, worked as caretakers in the Smokies as well as volunteering at ATC headquarters. "Life would certainly be drab if we didn't have all these wonderful friends and activities associated with the AT. It has definitely kept my retirement from being boring."

Kathy Kelly Borowski went from almost no self-confidence and self-esteem to more than she could possibly imagine. "I even accepted the fact that I was going to be alone. I built a log home, my dream house, while I was single and acted as my own general contractor. That is how I met my husband. I did not get married until two months after my 35th birthday. I've even managed to get my husband out on long distance backpacks and he had never camped before I met him." Since completing her hike, Kathy has hiked the Long Trail, the John Muir Trail, hiked to the bottom of the Grand Canyon, and spent two weeks in the backcountry of Alaska. She followed her dreams.

Future thru-hiker, Connie Salzarulo, Gladrags, shares that hiking gives her a chance to test her mettle, to gauge her strength, and to see if she can make it to a predetermined point in the data book. She challenges herself to survive in the woods with basic needs free from many of the things of our civilized world. "I feel smug when I get home and dress up for church or a special occasion and realize that yes, that dressed up, made up, hair done girl is me, but so too is the dirty, sweating, no makeup, straight haired, tick bitten Woman of the Woods! I celebrate them both and I'm glad to be both. I'm just so thankful I found that 'hiker trash' girl." When Connie gets anxious while hiking, she reminds herself that she chose to do this and gives herself permission to get off the Trail at the next road crossing or even never go hiking again. She knows that won't happen, but it helps at the time.

Dot MacDonald, D-Train, is a teacher like her best hiking buddy and sister, Barbara DiGiovanni, D-Boss. "Since I was a small child the

153

sight of a path leading into the forest brought with it an indescribable urge to follow its winding way. I have felt actual physical pain when I am unable to go even when I have followed that very path to many destinations and favorite spots a dozen times before. The pleasure of actually walking with my pack on feels just as thrilling as my first solo hike some 30 years ago. As I section hike the Trail, the experience and expectation of 'new trail' still holds me fast. I savor every turn and break and bead of sweat. I exult in the sweet feeling of the shelter roof and the tentsite signs. I think this will never pale and I am so grateful for this gift. It is all the more sweet when I can share it with my sister and my son which I do less than I wish, but it makes it all the more pleasurable when they are there. Just the sight of my half filled pack leaning against my living room wall is a sweet sight."

"So long after thru-hiking now," writes Cleo Wolf, Footloose, "I still feel empowered by the experience but less physically than I did back then. Today I feel it in the way I stand on the earth. When my feet touch the ground, they are connected to a great and powerful being who lives and breathes as we do and is aware as we are. And when I walk among the trees, I hear them sigh and know how deep their roots are, how tall their branches. The breeze brings to me pictures of meadows and woods, the birds tell me what has been happening in the world. The rocks pulse with life. I am at home on the earth, part of the world as never before. And my body remembers; when I walk I feel it. Starting is tentative, then a little more confident, then rolling along. My stride lengthens and the exuberance comes back. It is a pleasure to walk the earth."

Advice to Future Thru-hikers

DJ McCulloch- "Some people dream about climbing mountains. Others stay awake and do it."

"There aren't too many things I would change about my hike if I had to do it over." Rachel Dubois, Solophile, would try, however, to stay a little bit more independent throughout the hike. "At times, I felt some pressure to stay with certain people because I didn't want to hurt anybody's feelings or lose special friendships. Forming close friendships is a wonderful aspect of a thru-hike, but I'd just like to have been more true to myself and my desires in how I wanted to hike. I compromised my hike just to 'smooth the waters.' In hindsight, if they were truly good friends worth hanging on to, they would have understood my desires and my needs."

Kelly Winter, Amazin' Grace- "Don't buy into ideas that because you're a woman you can't do something. You can do whatever you want to do. Think of Grandma Gatewood. If she could hike the Trail at age 68, alone, wearing KEDS and using a drawstring laundry sack for a pack, then you can, too."

Carolyn Cunningham, Tawanda- "Follow your heart and hike your own hike. You will probably come into contact with people who will try to tell you what you should and should not be doing. You will have experiences that will change the way you look at the world. You will also have experiences that will make you want to get off the Trail. Make yourself work through it and find out what works best for you. While preparing, talk to as many different people as possible in order to get a broader perspective. There are many ways to hike the Trail. Your way will be best."

Carolyn also suggests having all your own gear. "It is your hike and having to make decisions with another can infringe upon your own experience. You can always choose to mail a tent ahead if you are sharing with another hiker. But, if you become too reliant on someone, you may realize halfway into your hike that you should have gone your separate ways. It is also ok to change your plans. If you start with someone and decide not to finish with him/her, that is better than being miserable the whole time. How many times are you going to hike the Trail? So when looking for a partner, don't forget to discuss plan B-what if we break up?"

Donna Tovey- "Do it." She described her hike as a life changing experience that strengthened her self-esteem and self-confidence.

Regina Erskine, Whispering Pine- "I had to return to my teaching job in the fall and couldn't take as much time as I would have liked to hike the AT. If I had had a longer time frame, I believe I would have been able to relax and enjoy my hike more. I still had a wonderful experience, but I would recommend to future thru-hikers, if possible, to give themselves a large amount of time, to hike their own hike and complete their journey at a pace that is best and most fulfilling for them." Regina was on a year's sabbatical from her teaching position and could start her thru-hike in the spring.

Sarah Dixon- "Be smart! Live it, love it, breathe it all in and don't miss one experience no matter how large or small. It will be unlike any other time in your life and will not be duplicated. It will warm your soul, fill your heart, blister your feet, and at times, challenge your courage and spirit, but you will realize the best that life can offer is on a simple day's hike."

Diane Myers, Jingles '97 and '98- "Just go out there and do it one step at a time." Diane feels she is a better richer person from hiking the Trail. Life can be simpler and like many women, she expressed feeling closer to God.

Donna Horn offers both practical and motivational advice. "If I were to do it over again, I would do the first two weeks with very low mileage; maybe even take the approach trail in two days. This way my body would have a chance to get in shape and acclimate to the terrain. The mountains in Georgia are not a piece of cake! My most serious injuries were tendonitis and bone bruises on the bottoms of my feet. Having adequate padding in the bottom of my boots and taking the first two weeks more slowly would have helped immensely."

"Go do it," Donna writes. "Don't sit there paralyzed with fear. Don't wait for someone to come along who will move your inertia. Don't wait for someone else's dreams to formulate the plan. Waiting for someday won't make it happen. If you are ready to go now, GO. The future will create more excuses why not. Three years after I hiked the AT, I broke my hip; I may still be able to do it again some day, but it will be a lot harder. It would certainly make it a big hurdle if I'd never done it before. You've got a lot more resources within yourself than you realize."

Anne Mausolff, The Green Mountaineer- "Prepare-physically and mentally. If you really want to do it, do it in whatever way you can, in whatever way you want. It's your life. It's your hike." Anne, a wise woman with extensive outdoor experience, highly recommends two books:

<u>Women's Bodies, Women's Wisdom</u> by Dr. Christiane Northrup and <u>The New Nutrition</u> by Dr.Michael Colgan.

Kathy Cummins, Fruitcake, suggests taking pictures, keeping a journal, and recording names and addresses of special people.

Joyce Johnson, Pilgrim's Progress, stresses the importance of drinking enough water. "When I started out I was not drinking enough water because I had to stop and take off my pack to reach it. This was a mistake. After having the experience of running out of water and facing near dehydration and heat exhaustion, I bought two more water bottles, one to go in my pack, the other that hooked on my belt where I could reach it."

Joyce also has had some serious bouts with poison ivy and poison oak. "I have scars from it and my eyes and ears have been swollen shut. I am much more afraid of it than I am of snakes, by a long shot." Because of her sensitivity to poisonous plants, Joyce had a series of three shots before her hike even though the doctor warned her of possible bad side effects. She had none and recommends that women check this out if they have a similar history of sensitivity.

"Know yourself and your strengths and limitations pretty well before you go. If you are prone to blisters, afraid to be by yourself, have trouble with periods, and can't lift too much, then work on these things ahead of time. Plan and prepare your trip, your body, and most of all, your inner strength. You can train like an athlete for the physical part of hiking, but if you aren't prepared psychologically and spiritually, you may not be strong enough to endure the physical part or deal with loneliness."

Cindy Miller, Mrs. Gorp- "Follow your dreams...you CAN do it...it just takes one step at a time."

T. Whittaker, Luna- "If it calls you, answer the call. Just do it. There is nothing to fear. I think the biggest fear would be to look back at my life and regret that I didn't follow my dreams and live my life to the fullest. Live your dreams. Listen to the voices in your head telling you to do something which at first may seem a bit crazy."

Kay Cutshall, The Old Gray Goose, followed her mother's advice. "I really feel when opportunity knocks we have to be listening because it may not knock again. My mama used to say you only live once but if you do it right, once is enough. Sometimes things are left standing in our way. We have to decide if they are going to keep us from moving on toward our goal or do we have to work on them to be able to set them aside. No matter what the outcome, three months on the Trail or a completed thru-hike, you will be proud of your accomplishment. To never step out and try to follow through on our dreams, goals, and wild thoughts when we have an opportunity is when we really fail to live our life to the fullest. All we dreamed or thought about is an accomplishment that fills our life with memories held dear forever. We alone are responsible for our own happiness; even though those around us can enhance it they are not the ones responsible for it."

Kay Wood suggests hiking for the pure enjoyment, for the sheer wonder of being alive to enjoy nature in its changing seasons, for the complete freedom to stop or go as you wish. Kay encourages women to consider combining hiking with Trail maintenance and personally gets much pleasure from this volunteer effort. Most hikers realize that without the hard work and dedication of the thousands of Trail maintainers volunteering through their individual hiking clubs along the length of the Trail, they would have no Trail to enjoy.

Novice hiker, Karen Bouknight is planning a thru-hike in the near future with her husband. She has outlined her plan, reiterating many of the points already discussed and suggests it might be useful for others. "If thru-hiking is your dream, there are several things you need to do to be successful even before you buy your equipment. The first thing you need is deciding why you want to thru-hike. What are your goals? Once you've decided that, WRITE THEM DOWN. Only about 5% of people even have goals, and even fewer write them down. You can't just keep the idea in your head. You have to write it down and put it where you can see it every day. Second, you have to attach deadlines to your goals. 'Someday' is not a deadline. At least select a month and year to start your hike. You can refine it to a specific day later. Third, develop a mental picture of yourself achieving your goal. Cut out pictures from hiking magazines and put them on the refrigerator. Do whatever it takes to help you visualize your goal. Fourth, you need to develop a plan. Planning a thru-hike is very extensive.

Before you can develop a good plan you need knowledge. Knowledge is gained in three ways: reading books/magazines about hiking, associating with people who have done what you want to do or mentoring with someone, and experiencing things yourself. It's best to read and associate first. Read something that will help you with your dream everyday. Finally, you need to set up checkpoints or milestones on your way to your goals and evaluate them periodically. If you are not doing the little steps to achieve your major goal, you'll never realize your dream."

Lisa Price, The Three Amigos, recalls a phone conversation she had when first inquiring about the Trail. "I remember a long, long time ago, I called a man to ask about the Trail. I later realized I'd been talking to Wingfoot. He told me that the Trail would be a touchstone, something used to measure all other experiences. I didn't understand that then. Completing the Trail is about faith in yourself, and confidence in yourself. I'm proud of how hard I can try. But I'm even prouder of how hard I can keep trying, my will I guess. Like steel, using heat and cold, my will was forged on the Trail. And yet although the Trail is about your own strength, it also prepares you for future relationships and friendships. There's a line from Hamlet that sums this up for me: 'This above all, to thine own self be true, and it must follow, as the night the day, thou canst not then be false to any man.'"

Good Luck and Happy Trails to all women who search to discover on the Appalachian Trail.

Conclusion

Eighty-four year old Margaret Thomassan responded to the survey and questionnaire. She is a member of the Appalachian Trail Conference and The Happy Hikers, a women's group within the Natural Bridge Appalachian Trail Club in Virginia. The members hike every Thursday and maintain a section of Trail. Attending summer camp in New Hampshire as a child, Margaret hiked a number of mountains in the Whites and knows what it is like sleeping on the ground in the open. She has hiked all 88 miles of the Trail her club maintains at least once. "I am very interested in the book you are writing and I hope to get one for my oldest granddaughter when it is printed. The approach is a grand one and that is needed very much." Margaret, thank you for your support and appreciating the nature of this collaborative women's effort.

Hikers generously contributed to this project by actively participating in several ways: through the WATL, the on-line Women's Appalachian Trail List, or by returning the survey and answering the questionnaire that was sent to hundreds of women throughout the country. They realize the significance of their input in continuing to educate themselves, each other, and girls and women searching to find the confidence to take that first step on the Appalachian Trail.

Personal notes from Rosie:

About the Trailside PBS Production

Before Wingfoot started his Trailplace website, the main internet research site I visited was the backpacker file on America On Line. Sometime during the winter preceding my hike I read an e-mail to perspective March-September south-north thru-hikers asking who would be willing to participate in a Trailside production scheduled for the 1995 thru-hiking season. Just like the decision to thru-hike made after two days of backpacking, I intuitively knew that I had to write a letter and give it a shot. It is just this intuitive sense that we need to listen to and trust. It would have been so easy to ignore that e-mail and think I would never be chosen and question whether anyone would be interested in seeing and hearing my Trail observations. However, I had already decided to do motivational speaking for women even before I had set one foot on the Trail and this opportunity was meant to be in my path.

I was asked to send a video so I found a videographer, Dick Gosselin, a local radio and TV news reporter, in the yellow pages. He filmed a 17 minute one take presentation and tells of my planning process as I sat in a Kennedy rocker in front of a blazing fire. The snow was still on the ground in Maine and I hadn't yet made all the final decisions concerning gear and equipment.

After acceptance to the future program, David Conover, the Trailside producer, came to my home several times. David's company, Compass Light out of Camden, Maine, specializes in videotaping unique adventures all over the world. He filmed some pre-hike insights including a humorous entry of me struggling to pack my down sleeping bag into a compression sack. The first attempt at packing my backpack at home took 4 ½ hours. Needless to say, that was greatly reduced as the hike progressed

161

and, except for the early and late parts of the hike, I was on the Trail packed and hiking between 6 and 6:30 a.m. every morning. David camped on Springer filming me at the summit on March 13th as well as a number of other hikers passing through in that time period. He subsequently, over the next seven months, met the various hikers at intervals although we also filmed ourselves on occasion while carrying a small camera and tripod.

David often coordinated his trips to meet hikers when we got to towns or called him from a roadside phone when we had the opportunity. Taking a cell phone would have been entirely out of the question. Once after a tiresome wait for a lift into Slatington, Pennsylvania, I ran into David at an ATM machine. I had planned on spending the night in town doing laundry and re-supplying. He knew I was in the area from previous shelter register entries and wanted to shoot that day. He treated me to lunch and we headed out to Lehigh Gap, a steep rocky ascent I had hoped to attack when rested the following day. That entry turned out to be one of the more personally poignant entries as I mentioned the concept of being "enough" and questioned what it would take to feel satisfied with myself and my accomplishment. David is like a gazelle and scrambles effortlessly over all types of terrain. We descended, I did my chores in town, and the following day again ascended Lehigh Gap but this time just continued on.

The Trailside show chose me to be the hiker to meet John Viehman, the host, at the halfway point. I gained a tremendous respect for the tedious nature of film production as we did take after take. The production was unscripted so we added, subtracted, and improved on each take. It was a fascinating process and most of what was filmed was never used. At noon we broke for a picnic for the production crew and ATC staff on the lawn beside the headquarters in Harper's Ferry. That day as well as the whole process was fun, educational, and rewarding and a real highlight of my thru-hike.

The production was first aired around Thanksgiving of 1995. It is still being aired 4 years later. I am touched by the comments and reactions to this two part Trailside show and am grateful that I had the insight to say "yes" in answering to that original e-mail and "yes" to staying in touch with David along the way so ultimately I was one of the five hikers featured in

162

the program. It would have been easy to say no just as it would have been easy to say no to thru-hiking. We already have the answers inside of ourselves but sometimes need a little prompting for them to come out.

A Final Thought

As a Maine native exposed to the woods and lakes as a child, it does not surprise me that I feel most at peace hearing the loons and smelling "the scent of the fragrant pine." In the early 60's, when I was a teenager, my father built a camp inaccessible by road on a pond north of Caratunk. This tiny town with about 100 residents is a few days' hike south of Monson and the 100-mile wilderness, the last stage of a northbound thru-hike. Between Caratunk and Monson is Moxie Bald, on a clear not too windy day, my favorite spot on the whole AT. On the many drives north toward Jackman over the years I learned of Benedict Arnold's ill-fated attempt to capture Quebec. I remember the logs floated down the river, a practice the paper companies ceased years ago, and saw the subsequent development of white water rafting companies. But I never heard how the Appalachian Trail crosses the Kennebec and the road we drove to camp. Maybe I wasn't listening.

The challenge of the AT was not in my realm of awareness as I searched for adventure, traveling, working, and exploring for many years in other countries. We sometimes search further afield when what we need to find is right here at home...literally under our feet. While still compiling material for this book, I went up to camp. It was still as peaceful and uncrowded on the pond as it was in the 60's and I stopped on the way to visit the Caratunk General Store and Kennebec River crossing. I sent Wingfoot a postcard of Steve Longley, the Kennebec ferryman, and asked Marie Beane, the postmistress and storeowner, to make sure it got a Caratunk postmark.

Up at camp, Janice, my youngest sister and main support team member during my thru-hike, joined me in the boat as we looked for loons listening for their distinctive cry and searched for signs of the leaves starting to turn. Fall comes early in the north country. We puttered along enjoying the calm surface and the late summer season without black flies and mosquitoes. Over the years we've collected fossils along the shore, fished the pond, trapped 4 inch long crayfish "racing" them on the floor, seen moose and bear wandering in front of the camp, collected branches gnawed by beaver, and gone berry picking in secret spots. We walked the beach looking for interesting pieces of driftwood, immersed ourselves in novels, put on plays for each other, and our evening's entertainment was the sunset over the western mountains and a game of scrabble. The Maine woods provided the backdrop.

Recently, buried under some old tackle boxes in the fish closet in the basement of our childhood home, Janice discovered a carton of photographs belonging to my late father, an avid Maine outdoorsman. We then realized that during the 30's he worked for the CCC, the Civilian Conservation Corps, and the photos pictured work crews in the woods. The final stage of the Appalachian Trail making the AT continuous from Georgia to Maine was completed in 1937 by the CCC and is commemorated with a stone plaque on the Trail in Maine. I'd like to think that my father was a member of that trail blazing team or at least was aware of this historic project. Maybe he knew that in my own way and in my own time, I would find the Appalachian Trail by myself when I most needed it.

CONTRIBUTORS

Joy Aarsvold-Misselt, Rhenda Acton, ("Amazon Queen"), Molly Ames, Annie Anderson ("Grannie Annie"), Nancy Anderson, Susanne Wright Ashland, Jean Arthur (1/2 of the "Meanderthals"), Jane Atkinson ("Leadfoote"), Edna Baden, Betty Lou Bailey, Cynthia Barnett, Lisa Barter ("Tinkerbell"), KarenBerger, Linda Bertoncini, Dana Berthold, Patricia Blackmon, Meoldy Blaney ("Midnite"), Deborah Blick ("Cricket"), Roberta Blick ("Mama Cricket"), Sue Bodyke, Sarah Boehm, Kathy Kelly Borowski, Karen Borski ("Cookie/Nocona"), Dee Boucher, Karen Bouknight, Bitsy Bredimus, Zaz Breisford ("Sunbeam"), Barb Briggs, Amy Buonassi ("Sweet Magnolia"), Charme Burns ("Gypsy Mama"), Connie Cabe ("Muddy"), Rhonda Campbell, Kate Canney ("Mallow"), Celia Carlen, Elaine Carlson ("Pilot"), Carol, Diana Cascioli ("Raven"), Laura Charlotte, Leslie Clapp ("Flower Power"), Amy Clark, Anni Clark, Martha Clark, Amity Clifford ("Dutchboy"), CMS, Jean Cooley, Karen Couch ("Hobbling Fool"), Robyn Crispe ("Critter"), Leslie Croot ("Squirrel"), Sylvia Crump ("Orange Blossom Mama"), Cathie Cummins ("Fruitcake"), Carolyn Cunningham ("Tawanda"), Kathleen Cutshall ("Old Gray Goose"), Jean Deeds ("Indiana Jean"), Julianne Delzer, Shannon Dewshyn ("Dewshine"), Barbara DiGiovanni ("D-Boss"), Hazel Diller, Meg Diviney ("Yoda" of the Cheese Girls), Sarah Dixon, S. Dodge, Carol Donaldson ("Coosa"), Jeannette Donlon, Mary Dotson, Sandra Downs, Sasha Drew, Rachel DuBois ("Solophile"), Jane Dudley, S. Dulles, Meredith Dunker, Trudy Eagan, Dania Egedi ("Lightweight"), Debby Emerson ("Dogmother"), Regina Erskine ("Whispering Pine"), Marcia Fairweather ("Almost There"), K.C. Felton, Carey Fields ("Pennsylvania Rose"), Lea Filippi, Jeanne B. Fisher, Laurel Foot ("Happy Feet"), Rebekah Fowler, Gail M. Francis ("gmf"), Sena Frank, Sue Freeman ("Blueberry"), Teresa French, Amy Friends, Shari Galvez ("SecondChance"), Julie Garcia, Cheryl Gaudreau ("Soulmates"), Laurel Gess ("Mountain Laurel"), Linda Gibbons, Ellen Gibson ("Steadfast Buffalo"), Ana Gipe, Pam Glass ("Flamingo"), Amanda Godino("LambThiel"), Anita Golton ("Thistle"), Gratham, Lisa Groshong, Stephanie H., Karyn Hahn, Joyce Haines, Kristin

Hanson, Katherine Hasse, Pat Hatton ("Mad Hatter"), Nellie Hayse ("Snoopy"), Stacy Louise Heiliger, Amanda Henck,Stephanie Hiller, Donna Hoffman, Cheryl Hoover, Lindsay Hoppes, Donna Horn, Barbara Horsfall, Elizabeth Hoster ("Liddy"), Beth Hronek, Beverly Hugo ("Maine Rose"), Diane Hunsicker, Kathi Indermill, Michelle Irvin ("Mountain Laurel"), Linda Ivey ("Mountain Mama"), Lisa Jacobs, Mona Jackson, Linda Jagger, Gail Johnson ("Gutsy"), Joyce Johnson ("Pilgrims Progress"), T. Johnson ("Snowflake'), Sarena Johnstone , Carol Keck, W. E. Kendall, Sue Kennedy, Sue Kenn ("White Glove"), Karen Kent-Pyle ("The Dancing Bears"), Jan Kerns ("Tagalong"), Lori Kessler ("Dr. Daisy G"), Kelly Kidson, Ellen Kilpatrick ("Mama Kazoo"), Rosalea Kimball ("Wayan"), Jo-Ellen ("Mummyfoot"), Joan King, Peggy Kinnetz ("Mama Llama"), Suzanne Konopka("Doc"), Diane Kortan, Kathy Kovacic, Barb Kreider, Carla Lafleur, Jeanne Lajoie, Stephanie LaMastra, Barbara Landis, Michele Landis, Hilary Lang ("Weatherwoman'),Vivian LeBlanc), G. Lewis, Kerstan Lincoln ("Skylark/Space Girl"), Sherry Lizotte, Ann Lockhart, Susan Lohnes, Victoria Logue, Lynn, Dot MacDonald ("D-Train"), Joyce Mailman ("Espy"), Malmquist, Courtney Mann ("Mojo"), Martha Manzano ("Gypsy"), Anne Mausolff ("The Green Mountaineer"), D.J. McColloch, Joan McFadden ("Nine"), Lynne McKee, Vicki McMahan, Kathryn Mehlenbacher, Cynthia Miller ("Broken Arrow"), E. Minor, Linda Moak ("Red Rainbow"), Molly GypZ, ("Momma Turtle"), Bethann Morgan, Diane Myers ("Jingles"), Jennifer Neumann ("Tonic"), Leslie Niederstadt ("Annapurna"), Laurie Normand, Joan Norris ("Bluetrail"), Janet Offermann, Sharon Onge ("Zontian Granny"), Ginny Owen ("Spirit Walker"), K. Elaine Owens, Alisa O'Harra ("Pooombah"), S. Pabody, Ann Palaitis ("Seasons"), Kim Parent ("Trillium"), Tracy Parizek ("Oasis"), Julie Parker, Kimberly Parry ("Tigger"), Linda Patton ("Earthworm"), Rebecca Pat, Nancy Peach, Mary Pfennig ("Hoosier Mama"), Mary Pierce, Player, Elizabeth Potenza, Priscilla Potter ("Silly Potty"), C. L. Pruett, Raborn, Danyele Read, Emily Reith ("Bugbite"), Jacquelyn Reith, Joanne Renn, Jo Reynolds, Tammy Richards ("AT Gracie"), Brooke Robertshaw ("River"), Christy Robertson ("Truffle"), Sawnie Robertson ("Kinnickinic"), Dolores Roberts ("Downhill Hopeful"),

Donna Roberts, Nancy Robinson ("Slim"), Kate Robson, Kimber Rogers, Karen Rogers ("Wren"), Judy Root, Mary Sue Ross-Roach ("Southern Harp"), Susan Roquemore ("The Dragon Lady"), Connie Salzarulo ("Gladrags"), Mary Sands ("Mama Boots"), Donna Brigley Savluk ("Ward's Girl"), Stacy Scheel ("Steady On"), Bunny Sneider ("Mother Superior"), Joyce Scott, Pat Shannon, Susan Shaver, Christine Shaw ("Firefly"), Melissa Shook, Illah Sink ("Sunflower"), H. Slunt, Larissa Smith, Debbie Smith ("Twilight"), Hope Smith, Kip Smith (1/2 of the "Pink Panthers"), Larissa Smith, Kyra Sotter ("Purple Haze"), Verna Soule ("Gran'ma Soule"), Karen Sousa, Jeanne Spellman, Lee Spengler, Kristin St. James ("The Wanderer"), Emma Stephens, N. Stetson ("Morning Glory"), Nancy Stoltzfus, Jeanette Stoner ("Double Crust"), Melissa Sumpter ("Selky"), Nan Sutton, Sherri Swartz ("Sunrise"), Tammi Sweet, Carolyn Thalman, Crystal Theesfeld ("Skeeter"), Margaret Thomasson, Audrey Thompson, Michelle Thompson-Ball, Debbie Tillman ("Dogmother"), Donna Tovey, Sandy Trimble, Mary Twitty ("Den Mama"), Stephanie Tyndall ("Fingerprint"), Grace Tyner ("Amazing Mama"), Janet Valine ("The Rockhoppers"), Beverly Valley ("Florida Slipper"), Patricia Vanderstelt, Kathleen Vann, Pat Villeneuve ("Give Me Chocolate"), Kristi Voelkerding, Katy Warner, Jennifer Whitcomb ("Yahoola!"), Donna White, Linda White, T. Whittaker ("Luna"), Sue Williams ("Leapfrog"), Cinda Williamson ("Timmy"), Asha Williams ("Footprints"), Edna Williams, Sue Williams ("Leapfrog"), T. Williams, Naoma Wilson ("Grundoon"), Jennifer Winn ("Pace Maker"), Kelly Winters ("Amazin' Grace"), Cleo Wolf ("Footloose"), Kay Wood, Missy Wood, Coral Worth, Debi Young ("Running Water"), L. Zachanewicz, and those who chose to remain anonymous.

In addition to the women who actually contributed to the book through responding to surveys and questionnaires, other individuals provided support in a myriad of other ways. A warm thank you to Ruth Smith and Nancy Lippard of Hot Springs who welcomed me into their home for two weeks during the '98 Trailfest celebration with their generous southern hospitality. Section hiker, Mickey Pellillo, Broken Boot, was

167

sitting enjoying herself in the Smokey Mountain Diner when she was willingly roped into folding and stuffing envelopes with surveys and questionnaires. Father Vince, Father George and Father Joe provided a safe haven for contemplation and creativity. Jane Marriott, Pokey, drove through the night from Indiana to spend a few days in the reception room of the local Presbyterian Church in Hot Springs compiling the list of contributors from scads of note cards, endless e-mails, and piles of papers. Jane and Gail Johnson, Gutsy, relaxed on Wingfoot's porch, read through the initial draft and provided excellent feedback and camarderie. To all the hikers who have hosted me in their homes, made suggestions on-line or in person, and invited me to share my AT thru-hike with their groups, thank you for your support and confidence.

A very special thank you is in order for Linda Patton whose bibliography is also found on the trailplace website. Linda, Earthworm, has been a Reference Librarian at Florida State University's Strozier Library for 20 years. Mother of two and grandmother of one, she began backpacking (mostly solo) ten years ago at the age of 50 and has section-hiked over 300 miles of the Appalachian Trail. She is a maintaining member of the Florida Trail Association and creator/maintainer of a seven mile hiking trail in Tallahassee, Florida. Earthworm puts our Earth first and is a lover of critters and wild places.

Support the ATC:
Appalachian Trail Conference
PO Box 807
Harper's Ferry, WV 25425
Tel:(304)535-6331
http://www.atconf.org

BIBLIOGRAPHY

APPALACHIAN TRAIL- GENERAL

Adkins, Leonard. *The Appalachian Trail: A Visitor's Companion.* Birmingham, AL: Menasha Ridge Press, 1998.

Chase, Jim. *Backpacker Magazine's Guide to the Appalachian Trail.* Harrisburg, PA: Stackpole Books, 1989.

Emblidge, David. *The Appalachian Trail Reader.* New York: Oxford University Press, 1996.

Fisher, Ron. *Mountain Adventure: Exploring the Appalachian Trail.* Washington, DC: National Geographic Society, 1988.

Fisher, Ronald M. *The Appalachian Trail.* Washington, D.C.: National Geographic Society, 1972.

Luxenberg, Larry. *Walking the Appalachian Trail.* Mechanicsburg, PA: Stackpole Books, 1994.

Marshall, Ian. *Story Line: Exploring the Literature of the Appalachian Trail.* Charlottesville: University Press of Virginia, 1998.

Setzer, Lynn. *A Season on the Appalachian Trail: An American Odyssey.* Birmingham, AL: Menasha Ridge Press, 1997.

The Staff of "The Atlanta Journal-Constitution," et al. *Appalachian Adventure: From Georgia to Maine--A Spectacular Journey on the Great American Trail.* Atlanta, GA: Longstreet Press, 1995.

APPALACHIAN TRAIL- GUIDEBOOKS-GENERAL

Bruce, Dan. *The Thru-Hiker's Handbook.* 9th ed. Hot Springs, NC: Center for Appalachian Trail Studies, 1999.

Chazin, Daniel D. *Appalachian Trail Data Book.* 21st ed. Harpers Ferry, WV: Appalachian Trail Conference, 1998.

Edwards, Henry, ed. *Appalachian Trail Thru-Hiker's Companion.* 6th ed. Harpers Ferry, WV: Appalachian Trail Conference, 1998.

APPALACHIAN TRAIL- GUIDEBOOKS-SOUTH TO NORTH

APPALACHIAN TRAIL CONFERENCE SERIES:

Appalachian Trail Guide to North Carolina-Georgia. 11th ed. Harpers Ferry, WV: Appalachian Trail Conference, 1998.

Appalachian Trail Guide to Tennessee-North Carolina. 11th ed. Harpers Ferry, WV: Appalachian Trail Conference, 1995.

Appalachian Trail Guide to Southwest Virginia. 2nd ed. Harpers Ferry, WV: Appalachian Trail Conference, 1998.

Appalachian Trail Guide to Shenandoah National Park: With Side Trails. 11th ed. Vienna, VA: Potomac Appalachian Trail Club, 1994.

Appalachian Trail Guide to Central Virginia. 1st ed. Harpers Ferry, W V: Appalachian Trail Conference, 1994.

Appalachian Trail Guide to Maryland and Northern Virginia: With Side Trails. 15th ed. Vienna, VA: Potomac Appalachian Trail Club, 1995.

Guide to the Appalachian Trail in Pennsylvania. 10th ed. Cogan Station, PA: Keystone Trails Association, 1998.

Appalachian Trail Guide to New York-New Jersey. 14th ed. Harpers Ferry, WV: Appalachian Trail Conference, 1998.

Appalachian Trail Guide to Massachusetts-Connecticut: With Northern Berkshires and the Mohawk Trails. 10th ed. Harpers Ferry,WV : Appalachian Trail Conference, 1996.

Appalachian Trail Guide to New Hampshire-Vermont. 9th ed. Harpers Ferry, WV: Appalachian Trail Conference, 1998.

Guide to the Appalachian Trail in Maine. 13th ed. Augusta, ME: Maine Appalachian Trail Club, 1996.

EXPLORING THE APPALACHIAN TRAIL SERIES

Emblidge, David. *Hikes in Southern New England: Connecticut, Massachusetts, Vermont.* Mechanicsburg, PA: Stackpole, 1998.

Gove, Doris. *Hikes in the Southern Appalachians: Georgia, North Carolina, Tennessee.* Mechanicsburg, PA: Stackpole, 1998.

Kodas, Michael. *Hikes in Northern New England: New Hampshire, Maine.* Mechanicsburg, PA: Stackpole, 1999.

Lillard, David. *Hikes in the Virginias: Virginia, West Virginia.* Mechanicsburg, PA: Stackpole, 1998.

Scherer, Glenn, *Hikes in the Mid-Atlantic States: Maryland, Pennsylvania, New Jersey, New York.* Mechanicsburg, PA: Stackpole , 1998.

APPALACHIAN TRAIL-MEMOIRS

Blaney, Melody A., and L. K. Ullyart. *A Journey of Friendship: A Thru-Hike on the Appalachian Trail.* Marietta, OH: River Press, 1997.

Brill, David. *As Far As the Eye Can See: Reflections of an Appalachian Trail Hiker.* Nashville, TN: Rutledge Hill Press, 1990.

Browne, Robert A. *The Appalachian Trail: History, Humanity, and Ecology.* Stafford, VA.: Northwoods Press, 1980.

Carr, Pam and John. *Follow the White Blazes From Georgia to Maine: British Hikers' Views of the Appalachian Trail.* York: Appalachian Walks UK, 1993.

Coplen, Jim. *The Wild Birds' Song: Hiking South on the Appalachian Trail.* South Bend, IN: American Bison, 1998.

Cornelius, Madelaine. *Katahdin (With Love): An Inspirational Journey.* Lookout Mountain, TN: Milton Publishing Co., 1991.

Deeds, Jean. *There Are Mountains to Climb: An Inspirational Journey.* Indianapolis, IN: Silverwood Press, 1996.

Flack, James, and Hertha Flack. *Ambling and Scrambling on the Appalachian Trail.* Rev. ed. Harpers Ferry, W V: Appalachian Trail Conference, 1983.

Garvey, Edward B. *Appalachian Hiker II.* Rev. ed. Oakton, VA: Appalachian Books, 1978.

Garvey, Edward B. *The New Appalachian Trail.* Birmingham, AL: Menasha Ridge Press, 1997.

Hare, James R., ed. *Hiking the Appalachian Trail.* 2 vols. Emmaus, PA: Rodale Press, 1975.

Haszonics, Joe J. *Trail Days: Thru-Hikers on the AT.* Margate, FL: Minuteman Press, 1998.

Hurlbert, Sandy and Rodney. *Fred and Litefoot: Our Trek on the Appalachian Trail.* Estes Park, CO: Mountain Printery, 1995.

Illig, John. *Trail Ways, Path Wise: An Appalachian Trail Through-Walk.* Mt. Desert, ME: Windswept House, 1998.

Irwin, Bill. *Blind Courage.* Waco, TX: WRS Publishing, 1992.

Lowther, Mic. *Walking North.* Anchorage, AL: Lowther, 1990.

171

Women & Thru-Hiking on the Appalachian Trail

Ross, Cindy. *A Woman's Journey*. Harpers Ferry, WV: Appalachian Trail Conference, 1992.

Shaffer, Earl V. *Walking with Spring: The First Thru-Hike of the Appalachian Trail*. Harpers Ferry, WV: Appalachian Trail Conference, 1995.

Sherman, Steve, and Julia Older. *Appalachian Odyssey: Walking the Trail from Georgia to Maine*. Brattleboro, VT: Stephen Greene Press, 1977.

Wadness, Kenneth. *Sojourn in the Wilderness: A Seven Month Journey on the Appalachian Trail*. Prospect, KY: Harmony House Publishers, 1997.

APPALACHIAN TRAIL-PLANNING GUIDES

Bruce, Dan. *The Thru-Hiker's Planning Guide: Everything You Need to Know for Planning End-to-End Hikes on the Appalachian Trail*. Workbook ed. Hot Springs, NC: Center for Appalachian Trail Studies, 1995.

Curran, Jan D. *The Appalachian Trail: How to Prepare For and Hike It*. Highland City, FL: Rainbow Books, 1995.

Logue, Victoria, and Frank Logue. *The Appalachian Trail Backpacker: Trail-Proven Advice for Hikes of Any Length*. 2nd ed. Birmingham, AL: Menasha Ridge Press, 1994.

Whalen, Christopher. *The Appalachian Trail Workbook for Planning Thru-hikes*. 4th. ed. Harpers Ferry, WV: Appalachian Trail Conference, 1998.

APPALACHIAN TRAIL-VIDEOS

Deeds, Jean. *Life Lessons on the Appalachian Trail*. 1996. (VHS, 25 min.) Silverwood Press, 1508 E. 86th St., #105, Indianapolis, IN 46240.

Hogeboom, Thomas. *North to Katahdin on the Appalachian Trail*. 1992. (VHS, 28 min.) Thomas Hogeboom, R. R. 1, Box 460, Hardwick, VT 05843.

Moore, Carol. *Trail Magic: A Walkumentary*. 1991. (VHS, 75 min.) Carol Moore, P. O. Box 1875, Silverthorne, CO 80498.

Viehman, John. *Thru-Hiking the Appalachian Trail.* 1995. (VHS, 60 min.) Wellspring Media, 65 Bleeker St., New York, NY 10012.

Whelden, Lynne. *Five Million Steps: The Appalachian Trail Thru-Hiker's Story.* 1987. (VHS, 75 min.) Lynne Whelden Productions, 90 E. Union St., Canton, PA 17724.

Whelden, Lynne. *How to Hike the Appalachian Trail.* 1991. (VHS, 3 hrs.) Lynne Whelden Productions, 90 E. Union St., Canton, PA 17724.

BACKPACKING AND OUTDOOR SKILLS

Berger, Karen. *Advanced Backpacking: A Trailside Guide.* New York: W. W. Norton, 1998.

Berger, Karen. *Everyday Wisdom: 1001 Expert Tips for Hikers.* Seattle: Mountaineers, 1997.

Berger, Karen. *Hiking & Backpacking: A Complete Guide.* New York: W. W. Norton, 1995.

Campbell, Charles. *The Backpacker's Photography Handbook.* New York: Amphoto, 1994.

Curtis, Rick. *The Backpacker's Field Manual: A Comprehensive Guide to Mastering Backcountry Skills.* New York: Three Rivers Press, 1998.

Dlugozima, Hope, James Scott, and David Sharp. *Six Months Off: How to Plan, Negotiate, and Take the Break You Need Without Burning Bridges or Going Broke.* New York: Henry Holt, 1996.

Fletcher, Colin. *The Complete Walker III: The Joys and Techniques of Hiking and Backpacking.* 3rd ed. New York: Alfred A. Knopf, 1984.

Getchell, Annie. *The Essential Outdoor Gear Manual: Equipment Care & Repair for Outdoorspeople.* Camden, ME: Ragged Mountain Press, 1995.

Hall, Adrienne. *A Ragged Mountain Press Woman's Guide: Backpacking.* Camden, ME: Ragged Mountain Press, 1998.

Hampton, Bruce, and David Cole. *Soft Paths: How to Enjoy the Wilderness Without Harming It.* Rev. ed. Mechanicsburg, PA: Stackpole, 1995.

Harmon, Will *Wild Country Companion*. Helena, MT: Falcon Press, 1994.

Hart, John. *Walking Softly in the Wilderness: The Sierra Club Guide to Backpacking*. 3rd ed. San Francisco: Sierra Club Books, 1988.

Hoffman, Gary. *Hiking With Your Dog: Happy Trails*. 2nd ed. Merrillville, IN: ICS Books, 1997.

Hugo, Beverly R. *Women & Thru-Hiking on the Appalachian Trail- practical advice from hundreds of women long distance hikers*. Sevierville,TN: Insight Publishing, 1999.

Ilg, Steve. *The Outdoor Athlete: Total Training for Outdoor Performance*. 2nd ed. Evergreen, CO: Cordillera Press, 1989.

Logue, Victoria. *Backpacking in the '90's: Tips, Techniques & Secrets*. 3rd ed. Birmingham, AL: Menasha Ridge Press, 1995.

Logue, Victoria, and Frank Logue. *Stretching & Massage for Hikers & Backpackers*. Birmingham, AL: Menasha Ridge Press, 1994.

Manning, Harvey. *Backpacking: One Step at a Time*. 4th ed. New York: Vintage Books, 1986.

McGivney, Annette. *Leave No Trace: A Practical Guide to the New Wilderness Ethic*. Seattle: Mountaineers, 1998.

Meyer, Kathleen. *How to Shit in the Woods: An Environmentally Sound Approach to a Lost Art*. 2nd Berkeley ,CA: Ten Speed Press, 1994

Mueser, Roland. *Long-Distance Hiking: Lessons from the Appalachian Trail*. Camden, ME: Ragged Mountain Press, 1998..

Randall, Glenn. *Cold Comfort: Keeping Warm in the Outdoors*. New York, NY. Lyons Books, 1987.

Ridley, Tom. *Power Packing: Principles of Lightweight, Long Distance Backpacking*. 2nd ed. Murfreesboro, TN: 2LB Enterprises, 1996.

Ross, Cindy, and Todd Gladfelter. *A Hiker's Companion: 12,000 Miles of Trail-Tested Wisdom*. Seattle: Mountaineers, 1993.

Schneider, Bill. *Bear Aware: Hiking and Camping in Bear Country*. Helena, MT: Falcon Press, 1996.

Seaborg, Eric, and Ellen Dudley. *Hiking and Backpacking*. Champaign, IL: Human Kinetics, 1994.

Sierra Club. San Diego Chapter. *Wilderness Basics: The Complete Handbook for Hikers & Backpackers.* Edited by Jerry Schad and David S. Moser. 2nd ed. Seattle: Mountaineers, 1993.

Simer, Peter, and John Sullivan. *The National Outdoor Leadership School's Wilderness Guide.* New York: Simon & Schuster, 1995.

Smith, Cheryl S. *On the Trail with Your Canine Companion: Getting the Most Out of Hiking and Camping with Your Dog.* New York: Howell Book House, 1996.

Smith, Dave. *Backcountry Bear Basics: The Definitive Guide to Avoiding Unpleasant Encounters.* Seattle: Mountaineers, 1997.

Sumner, Louise. *Sew and Repair Your Outdoor Gear.* Seattle: Mountaineers, 1988.

Townsend, Chris. *The Backpacker's Handbook.* Camden, ME: Ragged Mountain Press, 1993.

Vonhof, John. *Fixing Your Feet: Preventive Maintenance and Treatments for Foot Problems of Runners, Hikers, and Adventure Racers.* Mukilteo, WA: WinePress Publishing, 1997.

Waterman, Laura, and Guy Waterman. *Backwoods Ethics: Environmental Issues for Hikers and Campers.* 2nd ed. Woodstock, VT: Countryman Press, 1993.

FIRST AID

Auerbach, Paul S. *Medicine for the Outdoors: A Guide to Emergency Medical Procedures and First Aid.* Rev. and updated ed. Boston: Little, Brown, 1991.

Breyfogle, Newell D. *Commonsense Outdoor Medicine and Emergency Companion.* 3rd ed. Camden, ME: Ragged Mountain Press, 1993.

Cordes, Ron, and Gary LaFontaine *The Cordes/LaFontaine Pocket Guide to Emergency First Aid.* [Rigby, ID]: Troutbeck and Greycliff Publishing Companies, 1993. Dist. by Umpqua Feather Merchants, Glide, OR.

Darvill, Fred T. *Mountaineering Medicine and Backcountry Medical Guide.* 14th ed. Berkeley: Wilderness Press, 1998.

Forgey, William W. *The Basic Essentials of First Aid for the Outdoors.* Merrillville, IN: ICS Books, 1989.

Forgey, William W. *The Basic Essentials of Hypothermia.* Merrillville, IN: ICS Books, 1991.

Forgey, William W. *Wilderness Medicine.* 4th ed. Merrillville, IN: ICS Books, 1994.

Gill, Paul G., Jr. *The Ragged Mountain Press Pocket Guide to Wilderness Medicine & First-Aid.* Rev. ed. Camden, ME: Ragged Mountain Press, 1997.

Isaac, Jeff. *The Outward Bound Wilderness First-Aid Handbook.* Rev. and updated ed. New York: Lyons Press, 1998.

National Safety Council. *Wilderness First Aid: Emergency Care for Remote Locations.* Boston: Jones and Bartlett, 1998.

Patient Care Publications. *Emergency Medical Procedures for the Outdoors.* 2nd ed., rev. Birmingham, AL: Menasha Ridge Press, 1995

Preston, Gilbert. *Wilderness First Aid.* Helena, MT: Falcon Press, 1997.

Schimelpfenig, Tod, and Linda Lindsey. *NOLS Wilderness First Aid.* 2nd ed. Harrisburg, PA: Stackpole, 1992.

Tilton, Buck. *Backcountry First Aid and Extended Care.* 2nd ed. Merrillville, IN: ICS Books, 1994.

Tilton, Buck. *Camping Healthy: Hygiene for the Outdoors.* Merrillville, IN: ICS Books, 1995.

Tilton, Buck, and Frank Hubbell. *Medicine for the Backcountry.* 2nd ed. Merrillville, IN: ICS Books, 1994.

Weiss, Eric A. *A Comprehensive Guide to Wilderness and Travel Medicine.* 2nd ed. Berkeley, CA: Adventure Medical Kits, 1997.

Wilkerson, James A., ed. *Medicine for Mountaineering & Other Wilderness Activities.* 4th ed. Seattle: Mountaineers, 1992.

FOOD

Axcell, Claudia, Diana Cooke, and Kikki Kinmont. *Simple Foods for the Pack.* Rev. ed. San Francisco: Sierra Club Books, 1986.

Barker, Harriett. *The One-Burner Gourmet.* Chicago: Contemporary Books, 1981.

Fleming, June. *The Well-Fed Backpacker.* 3rd ed. New York: Vintage Books, 1986.

Gray, Melissa, and Buck Tilton. *Cooking the One Burner Way: Gourmet Cuisine for the Backcountry Chef.* Merrillville, IN: ICS Books, 1994.

Jacobson, Cliff. *The Basic Essentials of Cooking in the Outdoors.* Merrillville, IN: ICS Books, 1989.

Kesselheim, Alan S. *Trail Food: Drying and Cooking Food for Backpackers and Paddlers.* Rev. ed. Camden, ME: Ragged Mountain Press, 1998.

Kreissman, Bern. *Eating Hearty in the Wilderness With Absolutely No Clean Up: A Backpacker's Guide to Good Food and "Leave No Trace Camping!"* Davis, CA: Bear Klaw Press, 1994.

Latimer, Carole. *Wilderness Cuisine: How to Prepare and Enjoy Fine Food on the Trail and in Camp.* Berkeley, CA: Wilderness Press, 1991.

Logue, Victoria and Frank Logue. *Cooking for Campers & Backpackers.* Birmingham, AL: Menasha Ridge Press, 1995.

Marrone, Teresa. *The Back-Country Kitchen: Camp Cooking for Canoeists, Hikers, and Anglers.* Minneapolis, MN: Northern Trails Press, 1996

McHugh, Gretchen. *The Hungry Hiker's Book of Good Cooking.* New York: Alfred A. Knopf, 1982.

MacManiman, Gen. *Dry It--You'll Like It!: A Book About Food Dehydration.* Updated ed. Fall City, WA: MacManiman, 1983.

Miller, Dorcas. *Backcountry Cooking: From Pack to Plate in Ten Minutes.* Seattle, WA: Mountaineers, 1998.

Miller, Dorcas. *Good Food for Camp & Trail: All-Natural Recipes for Delicious Meals Outdoors.* Boulder, CO:Pruett Pub. Co., 1993.

Pearson, Claudia, ed. *NOLS Cookery.* 4th ed. Mechanicsburg, PA: Stackpole, 1997.

Prater, Yvonne, and Ruth Mendenhall. *Gorp, Glop and Glue Stew: Favorite Foods From 165 Outdoor Experts.* Seattle: Mountaineers, 1982.

Spangenberg, Jean. *The Portable Baker: Baking on Boat and Trail.* Camden, ME: Ragged Mountain Press, 1997.

Viehman, John, ed. *Trailside's Trail Food*. Emmaus, PA: Rodale Press, 1993.

WOMEN OUTDOORS

Aspen, Jean. *Arctic Daughter: A Wilderness Journey*. Minneapolis, MN: Bergamot Books, 1988.

Aspen, Jean. *Arctic Son: Fulfilling the Dream*. Birmingham, AL: Menasha Ridge Press, 1995.

Berger, Karen. *Where the Waters Divide: A 3,000-Mile Trek Along America's Continental Divide*. New York: Harmony Books, 1993.

Bond, Marybeth. *Gutsy Women: Travel Tips and Wisdom For the Road*. San Francisco: Travelers' Tales, 1995.

Bond, Marybeth, ed. *Travelers' Tales: A Woman's World*. San Francisco: Travelers' Tales, 1995.

Gould, Jean, ed. *Season of Adventure: Traveling Tales and Adventure Journeys of Women Over 50*. Seattle: Seal Press, 1996.

Helmericks, Constance. *Down the Wild River North*. Boston: Little, Brown, 1968.

Linnea, Ann. *Deep Water Passage: A Spiritual Journey at Midlife*. Boston: Little, Brown 1995.

Maxwell, Jessica. *Femme D'Aventure: Travel Tales from Inner Montana to Outer Mongolia*. Seattle: Seal Press, 1997.

McCairen, Patricia C. *Canyon Solitude: A Woman's Solo River Journey Through Grand Canyon*. Seattle: Seal Press, 1998.

Niemi, Judith. *The Basic Essentials of Women in the Outdoors*. Merrillville, IN: ICS Books, 1990.

Rogers, Susan Fox, ed. *Another Wilderness: Notes from the New Outdoorwoman*. 2nd ed. Seattle: Seal Press, 1997.

Rogers, Susan Fox, ed. *Solo: On Her Own Adventure*. Seattle: Seal Press, 1996.

Ross, Cindy. *Journey on the Crest: Walking 2600 Miles from Mexico to Canada*. Seattle: Mountaineers, 1987.

Thayer, Helen. *Polar Dream*. New York: Simon & Schuster, 1993.

"Maine Rose" and daughter Saretta

Women & Thru-Hiking on the Appalachian Trail

Printed in the United States
21153LVS00007B/1-75